A YEAR OF FESTIVALS

A Year of Festivals

A GUIDE TO BRITISH CALENDAR CUSTOMS

Geoffrey Palmer and Noel Lloyd

WITH LINE DRAWINGS BY GARETH FLOYD
AND 24 PAGES OF PHOTOGRAPHS

FREDERICK WARNE

Published by
Frederick Warne & Co Ltd
London · England
1972

© *Geoffrey Palmer and Noel Lloyd 1972*

FOR

Brian Pike

ACKNOWLEDGEMENTS

The authors and publishers wish to thank The English Folk Dance and Song Society for its assistance in connection with the photographs, Brian Shuel for his advice on the text, and the following for their kind permission to reproduce photographs: The University of Reading, Museum of English Rural Life for Plate 1 (above); British Tourist Authority for Plates 1 (below), 10 (below), 12 (below), 16 (both), 22 (both) and 23 (above); Kathleen Mitchell for Plate 2 (above); John Gay for Plate 2 (below); Brian Shuel for Plates 3, 4 (both), 5, 6 (all three), 7 (both), 8 (both), 9 (below), 10 (above), 11 (below), 14, 17, 18 (below), 19 (below) and 20 (both); Keystone Press Agency, Ltd for Plates 12 (above), 19 (above) 21 (both), 23 (below) and 24 (both); IMF News for Plate 13 (below); Aberdeen Journals, Ltd for Plate 15; and The Bedfordshire Times for Plate 18 (above).

LIBRARY OF CONGRESS CATALOG
CARD No. 71–186754

CASED EDITION   ISBN: 0 7232 1309 7
PAPERBACK EDITION ISBN: 0 7232 1460 3

Printed in Great Britain by
William Clowes & Sons, Limited
London, Beccles and Colchester

Contents

List of Plates

7

Introduction

THE·British Isles are rich in customs and rites that are bound up with the changing seasons of the year and the rhythm of country life. Our islands have often been invaded in the past, and foreigners who have settled among us have brought with them their own customs which have gradually become part of our national heritage. But the weakening of community life, due to industrialisation, and the quickening tempo of progress have had a mutilating effect on folk observances that had lasted for hundreds of years with little change, and this is likely to happen still more as civilisation gallops on.

Fortunately, the British determination to cling tenaciously to habit and usage has prevented the complete extinction of the rites that our ancestors practised, and many are too deep-rooted ever to disappear altogether. Beneath the surface of modern life there are race memories, age-old rituals, and the need to propitiate the forces of nature, and they bubble up restlessly like a hot spring. Though they may break through with less spontaneity than they used to, an attitude to life that is linked to the elements of life itself must persist somehow, either as more or less vigorous survivals, or as revivals. Some modern revivals tend to be too artificial, but others have given a new vitality to old traditions. Unless folk customs are to be put under glass and kept in a museum, the latter must flourish.

It is said that if you scratch civilisation you find a savage. If you scratch the owner-occupier of a desirable semi-detached residence you will find a man who is unconsciously seeking something safe and familiar, something with roots deep in the forgotten past. He may call Morris dancers 'quaint', laugh at the idea of wassailing his apple trees and refuse to appear as St. George in a mummers' play, but he will still eat hot cross buns on Good Friday, hang up mistletoe at Christmas, and give a Hallowe'en party. He will hesitate to walk under a ladder, and will look at the weather forecast with more than ordinary interest on St. Swithin's Day. Modern man is what history has made him, and one facet of history lies in the popular customs that have their beginnings in cults almost as old as man himself.

To understand ourselves we must know what our ancestors did at work, play and worship. The source of that knowledge is often hidden in the seasonal rituals that sought to compel nature to obey man's will, to ensure fertility, to make the dark gods smile. The death of the sun in winter was mourned; its resurrection in spring was greeted with rejoicings. In spite of the distractions of the Space Age there is a vital need to look back occasionally and examine our links with pagan ancestors. If folk customs ever did die out there would be a loss of vigour, colour and diversity that an age of drab uniformity can ill afford.

The source of the original customs is clearly seen in Norse legends, Roman and Celtic cults, and in practices that were ancient before Christianity was born. There is evidence that as far back as Palaeolithic times men in caves were practising sympathetic magic. It was the Church, in its endeavour to stamp out what it considered anti-religious rites, that was largely responsible for their continuance. The early Christian fathers viewed with displeasure the wilful leanings of their converts towards the gods they should have discarded, but the wiser ones decided to face the struggle realistically. They allowed the old-established customs to remain, but under a veneer of Christianity. Pagan temples were purified with holy water, altars replaced idols, and Christian feast days were celebrated at the times of former pagan festivals. Gradually, though never completely, the supremacy of the old gods was overthrown. The underground resistance kept up the forbidden worship. When the Christian trimmings that decorate the great festivals of Easter, Whitsuntide and Christmas are stripped off, the older associations are revealed in their primitive and often savage nakedness.

This long and stubborn struggle between paganism and Christianity explains why most time-honoured customs are connected with the Church's calendar. The Church's influence on the life of the people, its importance as a centre of village life, and its own need for ritual have ensured that calendar customs have been observed in an almost unbroken sequence throughout many centuries; and always the heathen and religious elements have been closely intertwined. This has provided a fascinating field of study for folklorists and anthropologists, and for ordinary people who like to delve beneath the surface of this curious compound of folk art, history and religion.

The aim of this book is to explore the history of the customs and festivals of Great Britain which are connected with the calendar: those which lasted till recent times before succumbing to the march of progress, those which have survived two world wars, and those of a more recent origin which have some historical figure or great event as a focal point.

Customs which are still being observed are naturally of greater interest because they can be experienced personally, but those which are no longer celebrated are, apart from their value to historians, reminders that what once happened could happen again. It may be that in some places rudimentary memories of old rites still linger on, only needing the enterprise of village organisations to coax them back to life. There are still old men who are skilled in the making of corn dollies, others who remember the words of a mummers' play or the steps of a Morris dance. If the countryman's love of ancient things and his links with the circular movement of time could be re-established, modern life would be enriched by both simplicity and depth.

May

THE month of May represents the whole year in miniature as far as folk customs are concerned, for in May appear almost all the *dramatis personae*, the symbols, and the rituals that are found in the pagan festivals which centre round earth, fire, water, life, death and resurrection.

Although summer does not officially begin until June, May Day really marks its beginning. Much of the vitality of the old customs associated with the day in Europe, where it was the great rural festival of our forefathers, has disappeared, but folk memory, which dies hard, has kept a grip on the day, and people still practise the old rites with enthusiasm, even though they have little idea of the meaning behind them.

May Day celebrations had their origin in an ancient Roman Festival dedicated to Flora, the goddess of flowers and fruit, which was held annually from April 28th to May 3rd. The festival itself originated in even earlier myth and ritual, which perhaps go back to Palaeolithic times. Cave paintings give evidences of practices designed to propitiate the supernatural forces which controlled the fertility of the land and of animals, and of magic rites that would bring success in hunting. The cult of Flora was brought to Britain by Belgic invaders towards the end of the first century B.C. In later times Christianity took it over and adapted it to its own needs, but it never completely lost its pagan quality.

For hundreds of years, especially during the Middle Ages, it was the custom for all ranks of people, in both country and town, to go a-Maying early on May Day. As Herrick wrote:

> *There's not a budding boy or girle, this day,*
> *But is got up, and gone to bring in May.*

The young men and women rose soon after midnight, and to the sound of cows' horns and drums they went to the woods, where they broke down branches of trees and decorated them with bunches of flowers. We now celebrate May Day eleven days earlier than before the calendar was changed in 1752, and the hawthorn, the flower of May, is not likely to be blooming as profusely as it did on the old May Day. The girls bathed their faces in May dew to ensure a lovely complexion and to cure rheumatism, consumption and spinal weakness. Smaller girls, not so concerned about their personal appearance, made May garlands. They covered two hoops, one at right angles inside the other, with leaves and flowers, and sometimes they put a doll inside to represent the goddess of Spring. In some parts of the country it is still customary for groups of children to carry May garlands as they tour the streets of their village, singing: 'Good morning, lords and ladies, it is the first of May. We hope you'll view our garland, it is so very gay.' Then they hold out a collecting-box.

At sunrise the young people returned from the woods singing a carol, and they adorned cottage doors and windows with May blossoms and birch and larch boughs. Nettles and alder boughs were kept for unpopular villagers who disapproved of such goings-on.

The rest of the day was given over to various festivities. There was dancing on the village green, archery contests and exhibitions of strength. The highlight of the proceedings was the crowning of the May Queen, the human replica of Flora. By tradition she took no part in the games or dancing, but sat regally in a flower-decked bower and watched her 'subjects'.

In medieval times the Queen of the May was sometimes a youth dressed in white muslin decorated with ribbons. The Lord of the May, now rarely seen, but who was once as important as

the Queen, was also beribboned. Silk handkerchiefs were tied round his legs and arms, and he carried a sword. Spring itself was represented by a man who danced about inside a heavy frame which was completely covered with greenery. He was called Jack-in-the-Green or Jack-in-the-Bush; in other parts of Europe he was known as Green George, the Wild Man or Leaf Man. His name lives on in the sign boards of the many public houses called *The Green Man*.

Jack-in-the-Green can sometimes be seen in decorations and carvings found in many old churches, often as a face with leaves and twigs growing out of the mouth and ears. This strange character was adopted by chimney sweeps, whose annual holiday was on May Day. He was prominent in their processions, a single green figure covered with gaudy ribbons and tinsel among the black-faced sweeps.

One of the great features of May Day was the maypole, a tall, slim tree with all its branches lopped off. It was painted in various colours and was carried in procession, with musicians playing before it. It was erected on the village green or in the town market-place, where it was decked with garlands and flowers, and became the focal point of the festivities.

Philip Stubbes, a puritanical Elizabethan commentator, wrote: 'But their chiefest jewel they bring from thence is their maypole, which they bring home with great veneration, as thus: They have twenty or forty yoke of oxen, every ox having a sweet nosegay of flowers tied on the tip of his horns, and these oxen draw home this maypole (this stinking idol rather), which is covered all over with flowers and herbs, bound about with strings, from the top to the bottom, and sometimes painted with variable colours, with two or three hundred men, women and children following it, with great devotion. And thus being reared up, with handkerchiefs and flags streaming at the top, they strew the ground about, bind green boughs about it, set up summer halls, bowers and arbours hard by it. And then they fall to banquet and feast, to leap and dance about it, as the heathen people did, at the dedication of their idols, whereof this is a perfect pattern, or rather the thing itself.'

The Puritans believed that the maypole was a relic of paganism, and of course they were right. The old Saxons had worshipped an 'enormous pillar' called Irminsul, but long before their day the Romans had carried a similar symbol in procession during Flora's Festival. The tree had long been regarded as the most magnificent product of the vegetable world, and dancing round it was a mating rite, a plea for fertility. So the Puritans disapproved, and the gaiety and licence associated with the maypole came to an end during the Commonwealth, as did all May Day festivities. By an ordinance of the Long Parliament in 1644 all maypoles were taken down and removed by constables and churchwardens. Maypoles appeared again at the Restoration, however, and recovered much of their former popularity. In places which had supported the Cavaliers there was a tendency for the maypole to be dressed on May 29th, Restoration Day, rather than on May Day itself.

One of the earliest references to a maypole is found in a charter granted by King John to Cokersand Abbey, where it is called a 'mepul'; and there is a later reference in *A Midsummer Night's Dream*, when Hermia calls Helena 'a painted Maypole'.

Maypoles, which could be of pine, larch, elm, birch or ash, lasted for perhaps fifteen years, and were replaced only when the wood of the base became rotten. There are still places where the maypole is a permanent fixture, but in most villages which have them they are erected for seasonal festivals.

We have scanty information about exactly what dances were performed round the maypole, though *Sellenger's Round* is known to have been danced in Tudor times. Plaiting the maypole is a custom from southern Europe, where maypoles were shorter. It was introduced into England by John Ruskin. He started a May Day coronation ceremony at Whitelands Training College, and teachers took the continental style into their schools. The dances became pretty and ladylike, and lacked their former abandon.

The most famous maypole in England was erected in London in 1661, after the Restoration, on or near the site of a church called St. Mary le Strand. Pope refers to it in his *Dunciad*:

> *Amid that area wide, they took their stand,*
> *Where the tall Maypole once o'erlooked the Strand,*
> *But now, so Anne and Piety ordain,*
> *A church collects the saints of Drury Lane.*

The maypole in the Strand stood for over fifty years, an unusually long time, and was the last to be put up there. It was over 130 feet high, and was so heavy that it took twelve sailors, using pulleys and anchors, four hours to raise it, even though they were assisted by drums and trumpets. When the golden crowns, the many-coloured garland and the purple streamer at the top soared skywards the onlookers went wild with delight. The maypole remained there until 1717, when Sir Isaac Newton bought it as a support for a powerful new reflecting telescope which the French astronomer Huygens had presented to him.

Many London parishes had a maypole. A very old one, painted in bands of red and white, was set up before the south door of St. Andrew's Church in the City. It was so tall that the church became known as St. Andrew Undershaft. Between 1517 and 1552 it hung in Shaft Alley, under the eaves of a row of houses. It was taken down and sawn up after a local preacher had denounced it as a pagan symbol and called his congregation idol-worshippers.

May Day was principally a festival of youth, and in no part of it was youthful vigour more evident than in Morris dancing. This is a form of exercise, of pure peasant tradition, that reached the height of its popularity at the end of the sixteenth century, though it has survived, often by a single thread, to the present day. The tradition has been kept alive particularly in Oxfordshire, Gloucestershire, Warwickshire, Northampton-shire, Derbyshire, Cheshire and Lancashire.

Morris dancers usually make their first appearance on May 1st, emerge again at Whitsuntide, can be seen at country fairs and festivals all through the summer, and occasionally appear at Christmas with the mummers, with whom they have a close relationship. The present revival of Morris dancing is due in great part to Cecil Sharp, who saw his first Morris dance at Headington, near Oxford, on Boxing Day, 1899.

Morris dancing was once thought to be of Moorish origin, but that theory is no longer widely held. The genuine Moorish or Morisco dance was very different from the European Morris. It was often performed at puppet shows by a person dressed as a Moor, and it was considered significant that some English dancers blacked their faces, as the Bacup Coconut Dancers still do. The wide distribution of the dance in Europe, however, precludes a Moorish source. The face-blackening was a ritual disguise to hide the identity of the dancer.

It is possible that the Morris dance was first brought to England by Eleanor of Castile, the queen of Edward I, or by John of Gaunt in the time of Richard III when he returned from Spain; or it may have drifted over the Channel from France or Belgium, where it was performed at the beginning of the thirteenth century.

Robert Graves, in *The White Goddess*, considers that 'morris' was first written 'maris', and that Morris men were 'Mary's men'. He traces 'Mary' back to the ancient sea-goddess Marian, whom the Greeks called Aphrodite, and who can also be identified with the moon-goddess.

Sometimes, though, the simplest explanation may be the true one. The name 'morris' could have been imported from southern Europe and used for a dance already in existence in

England in the sense of 'pagan'. Thus 'Morris, or Moorish, dance' simply meant pagan dance.

Few traces of Morris dancing can be found before the time of the first Tudor kings, when churchwardens' accounts in several parishes show that it was a common feature of parish festivals. In the Cotswolds particularly, Morris dancing was an important part of the seasonal customs of country life up to the middle of the nineteenth century. When village communities began to break up during the Industrial Revolution Morris dancing gradually died out. Except in a few places it was almost forgotten by the end of that century.

The roots of Morris dancing stretch far back in antiquity, before the beginnings of organised religion, in the rites designed to celebrate the rebirth of spring, to ensure the safety of the harvest, the fertility of flocks and herds, and to propitiate the gods by ritual slaughter. All these things were embedded in the early culture of Northern Europe, and dancing gave expression to them.

Apart from the dancers, other characters were involved. Sometimes they joined the dance; often they did not. The Betty, Betsy or Moll was a man dressed as a woman, thus representing both sexes. The Fool carried a bladder on a stick and with it he struck both dancers and spectators. As a clown he acted as a link between them, but he was also the leader of the team—the 'Squire'.

The story of the Fool in history and religion is long, complicated and mysterious. He can sometimes be identified with the King-Priest who sacrificed and was sacrificed, sometimes with the Medicine Man who suffered death in order that the community should survive. His function was always concerned with death and revival, and there are traces of him in folklore which go back as far as the cult of Osiris in ancient Egypt.

The performers often included Jack-in-the-Green in his leafy cage; the Hobby-horse, half animal and half human, and a man with a beribboned sword on the end of which a cake was stuck. The cake was shared among the spectators and eaten for luck. This may have been originally part of a cereal sacrifice.

At the beginning of the sixteenth century the Robin Hood

Games, a kind of folk play, came into being and got mixed up with Morris dancing. The cast of the play included Robin Hood, a Christianised form of Robin Goodfellow, the god of witches; Maid Marian, who was perhaps associated with Marian the moon-goddess and was the forerunner of the May Queen; Friar Tuck and others of the Merry Men. Robin Hood was interchangeable with the Fool, and Maid Marian with the Betsy. During the play Robin Hood died and came to life again. This was intended to encourage the crops to grow and the summer to return.

The connection between the Robin Hood of the folk play and the outlaw of Sherwood Forest is difficult to establish. Perhaps when the fame of the ballad hero spread through the northern part of the country in the fifteenth century his name became attached to the old character of the Green Man.

Morris dances have very distinctive features. They are completely masculine, and are full of complex rhythms which demand perfect muscular control. The dancers stamp, kick and caper, though nowadays they do not expect their exertions to bring the crops out of the ground; and the bells which are attached to their costumes tinkle loudly, though not now to rouse the earth spirit or drive away evil demons. Some dances require staves or swords—the sacrificial instruments—and some need handkerchiefs. What was once a deadly serious fertility cult has become a mixture of healthy exercise and folk art.

Present-day Morris dancing is based on three styles, one found originally in the Cotswolds, one in Derbyshire, and the third in Lancashire. At Bacup in Lancashire the Britannia Coconut Dancers wear red and white skirts over black breeches. They black their faces and they hold wooden discs, made from bobbin tops, which they clap against similar discs fastened to their knees and waist. The Derbyshire dancers had larger teams, sometimes up to sixteen members and, though they were all men, one side danced as women with fancy hats and scarves, and their Betty was a black-faced witch. Cotswold dancers wear hats; they have bells on their trousers and dance with sticks or handkerchiefs in their hands. The side consists of six dancers;

the Fool or Hobby-horse, the Betty and the musicians are extras. The Bampton-in-the-Bush dancers are famous because they have inherited a living tradition which has been maintained from remote times without a break. The Headington Quarry Dancers, who wear cricket caps, have only been a little less long-lived.

Non-traditional teams of Morris dancers began when the English Folk Dance Society was formed by Cecil Sharp in 1911. In 1934 a federation of Morris Clubs, known as the Morris Ring, was established. It is most unlikely that this type of dancing will ever disappear again because it gains fresh impetus every year in schools, colleges and universities all over the country. Morris teams can be seen at Summer Festivals, in London Squares, on Tower Hill, at seaside resorts, in the Lake District, at Windsor, Stratford-on-Avon, Thaxted, Oxford and many other places, bringing folk art into modern life.

Sword dances were once part of folk plays, but the dramatic part of the performance has largely disappeared. Sword dancing remains, however, and is especially strong in the north of England, where the Danes introduced it from Europe. It was another part of the primitive festival which celebrated the struggle between the old year and the new, and is usually practised in winter. The ritual had to include first a sacrifice, then the victim's return to life. This killing (whether real or pretended) can be traced in the mimed beheading of the Fool in sword dances and in the death of the Turkish Knight in mummers' plays. The dramatic elements of the folk play are now shadowy fragments, and the characters of the Fool and his sons who are obliged to kill him are stylised and rudimentary. Even so, it is remarkable how, after all this time, sword dances give a vivid picture of man's oldest urge, the urge to survive, and of his belief that redemption can be obtained through sacrifice and resurrection. The 'plot' of the sword dance is also the story of Osiris, Tammuz, Adonis and Attis, a god of many names but of one character, who represented the yearly decay and revival of living things.

An interesting example of the remains of the folk play is a hilt-and-point sword dance of north-east England. The miners of Northumberland and Durham use a flexible steel sword with a handle at each end. This is called a rapper. The Rapper Dance consists of complicated figures in which the men are linked in a continuous chain by their swords. In Yorkshire the dancers use rigid steel swords with bare points, and the fishermen of Flamborough perform with wooden swords held in the left hand.

A significant feature of sword dances is the 'lock' or 'glass'— a point when all the swords are interlocked in a star formation. Sometimes the lock is held high to represent the sun, and the dancers move round it sunwise. Sometimes it is used to 'decapitate' the Fool. This is the climax of the dance, the ritual murder in the old folk play. The lock is placed round the Fool's neck and he is 'slain'. He comes to life again after a few moments and the next figure of the dance is performed. Again he meets death, and again wins survival, but he finally dies. He has been sacrificed to atone for the sins of others, and the health and strength of the family is ensured by his death.

At Grenoside, Sheffield, the dancers wear clogs and the leader has a rabbit-skin hat, worn with the head of the animal to the front. The hat rolls off when the lock is put round the leader's neck. After his 'decapitation' he is revived and rejoins the dance.

The Grenoside dancers' captain is also known as the Whiffler. He carries a curved sword and his job is to clear a space for the dancers and to drive away any evil spirits which may be lurking near by. The Whiffler of the Bampton Morris Dancers has become the sword-bearer, the man with the cake.

Though hints of the long-forgotten rites which were once part of the Spring ceremony can be discerned in all sword dances, today they are danced because they are vigorous and exciting, not for the sake of their magical significance.

May Day festivities were rounded off with the lighting of fires, especially in Scotland and Ireland, the north of England, Devon and Cornwall. This custom was of very ancient origin. It was once a sacrificial rite in the observance of Beltane, and was possibly connected with the old Celtic god Belenos, the 'bright fire'.

Bonfires were lit on the tops of hills, and sheep and cattle were driven through them to prevent disease in the coming year.

Young men leaped over the fires as much to show their skill as for any other reason, and women jumped across them to secure a husband or a safe delivery in childbirth. They danced round the fire sunwise to propitiate the god, and they ran about the fields with blazing torches to drive away witches.

These practices lasted in Scotland and Ireland up to the eighteenth century, but the simpler form of the ceremony, such as dancing round the fire, lasted for very much longer.

The pagan aspect of May Day has now disappeared. Only in a few places have traditional customs spanned the centuries without change, as fresh and wholesome as in the days when Beaumont and Fletcher could say:

For now the fragrant flowers do spring and sprout in seemly sort,
The little birds do sit and sing, the lambs do make fine sport;
And now the birchen-tree doth bud, that makes the schoolboy cry;
The Morris rings, while hobby horse doth foot it feateously;
The lords and ladies now abroad, for their disport and play,
Do kiss sometimes upon the grass, and sometimes in the hay. . . .
Up then, I say, both young and old, both men and maids a-maying,
With drums and guns that bounce aloud, and merry tabor playing!

Before setting out to attend the observance of an old custom, it would be wise to check the date and time with local authorities in order to save disappointment. Information can usually be obtained from the Town Hall, the Librarian or the Vicar.

May 1st   Magdalen College Tower,
May Morning Service   Oxford

At 6 a.m. the choir of Magdalen College assembles on the tower and greets the sunrise with the May Hymn, *Te Deum Patrem Colinus*, and other hymns appropriate to the day. The service ends with a peal of bells. The crowds watch from the street and from Magdalen Bridge, and afterwards there is Morris dancing in The High.

The ceremony is thought to have originated in a Requiem Mass for the soul of King Henry VII, though it is equally likely to have developed from a service that took place when the building of the tower was completed in 1501. When we remember, however, that in primitive times sun worship, together with various ritual acts, took place on high ground, it is more than possible that the memory of such a ceremony is enshrined in the present observance.

May 1st   Padstow,
Hobby-horse Festival   Cornwall

This festival, the relic of a Celtic May Day custom, is one of the most curious of all May Day festivities. The Hobby-horse, once so popular in May games, comes into its glory again. This is a weird figure, a man enveloped in a wooden hoop, six feet in diameter, draped with black tarpaulin, which emerges from the *Golden Lion* on May Day morning. The frame has a small horse's head at the front, and a wispy black tail behind, but the real head of the 'animal' is a devilish mask with a cruel snapping beak, hanging red tongue and tufts of fur. The mask is surmounted by a black and white pointed hat, with the inscription 'O.B.' on it—a simplified form of ''Obby'.

The Hobby-horse is accompanied by the Teaser, or Clubman, who wields a strange instrument called a club, but which is flattish and spade-shaped, more like bellows. His function is to tease the 'Oss into its traditional dance by waving his club before it and directing it on its rounds.

The 'Oss, with its retinue of singers, musicians and 'Doom Bar Pirates'—the Doom Bar is a bank of sand across the estuary of the Camel—sets off round the town to the lovely old folk tune called the Night Song, the chorus of which goes:

> *Unite, unite, let us all unite*
> (*For summer is acome in today*)
> *And whither we are going, let us all unite,*
> *In the merry morning of May.*

The 'Oss visits many houses, the occupants of which are serenaded with suitable verses of the Night Song and are wished good luck and happiness. At intervals the mood of the performance changes and the accordions play the slow, dirge-like Day Song—the words of which have lost any meaning they once had.

> *O where is Saint George?*
> *O where is he, O?*
> *He's down in his long-boat all on the salt sea O.*
> *Up flies the kite and down falls the lark O.*
> *There was an old woman and she had an old ewe,*
> *And she died in her own park O.*

During this song the 'Oss sinks to the ground as though it is about to expire, and the Teaser crouches before it and strokes its motionless snappers and head. Children pat it and tidy its whiskers, and the 'Oss soon revives. The Night Song starts up again and the 'Oss dances its way through the twisting streets, enticed by the Teaser.

During the 'Oss's peregrinations the crowd incites it to charge, with the mysterious cry of ''Oss, 'Oss, we 'Oss!' (possibly meaning 'to we', that is, 'to us') and the 'Oss responds by chasing, catching and engulfing pretty girls in its hood. 'Don't be frightened,' it says to them, 'it's lucky!' 'Luck', in this case, means plenty of children. The association between the covering-up of the maiden and a pagan fertility rite is clear. At one time the 'Oss would smear its captives' faces with tar or soot as part of the initiation process.

The 'Oss gambols through the town all day long, dying and reviving. The Night Song and the Day Song are sung alternately, money is collected, and a vast amount of beer is drunk. A second 'Oss, known as the 'Blue 'Oss' or the 'Temperance 'Oss', with its own Teaser, is also in evidence. In the evening the two 'Osses dance round the flame-capped maypole.

The spring rite in Padstow is another link with the familiar old drama, the theme of which is the death of the old year and its resurrection in the spring, though through the years it has gathered a number of overtones rooted in local associations. One of them is the story of how the crew of a marauding French ship was frightened away by a Hobby-horse when most of the men of the town were away fighting the French during the Hundred Years' War.

May 1st   Minehead,
Hobby-horse Festival   Somerset

The Hobby-horse of Minehead, which some call a ship, comes out on the evening of April 30th, and at sunrise on May Day. It visits Dunster Castle in the evening, and can be seen the two following evenings. The 'ship-horse' consists of a wooden frame about ten feet long which a man carries on his shoulders. The rest of his body is hidden by the canvas hanging from the frame. The material is decorated with circles of different colours, and coloured ribbons cover the upper part.

The head of the horse (or the mast and sails of the ship) is in the centre; and a long rope tail, once a real cow's tail, is fastened to the 'stern'. The man inside the contraption glides and sways through the streets, and sometimes swings his tail around anybody who refuses to contribute to the collecting-box.

Concertinas and drums now supply the music; formerly a tabor was used. Two 'gullivers' used to collect the money. They wore masks and conical hats and carried clubs. They disappeared after a disturbance one year when their 'right' to enter people's houses in search of a toll was challenged by an angry man who maintained that his home was his castle.

The ship form of the horse is said to date from 1772 when, on the evening before May Day, a ship sank in a storm off Dunster, three miles from Minehead. The only object to be washed ashore was a dead cow, the tail of which was used to decorate the horse. The Minehead Hobby-horse, therefore, is another example of how an old custom can lose much of its original symbolism. Nowadays the Horse makes occasional out-of-season appearances, and may be seen teasing August holiday-makers on the sea front as it makes its way to the cricket ground where the Minehead Show is held.

May 8th   Helston,
Furry (or Flora) Dance   Cornwall

The Helston Furry Dance which takes place on May 8th,
unless this falls on a Sunday or Monday, is the finest surviving
example of a celebration in which the whole town is *en fête*.
Everybody, from young children to grave local dignitaries,
takes part. The Furry Dance was once a pagan ritual but has
become associated with St. Michael, the patron saint of Cornwall
and of Helston. (May 8th is the Feast of the Apparition of St.
Michael.) At one time 'Furry' was thought to be a corruption
of 'Flora' and the dance itself inspired by the Floralia Festival,
but it is more likely to be a relic of a Celtic Spring festival which
formerly took place on May Day and was designed to welcome
the summer. 'Furry' probably comes from the old Celtic word
'fer', meaning 'fair'.

The origin of the name Helston is also in doubt. Hele-stone
(or Sun-stone) is a possibility; so is Hellstone, about which
there is a pleasant legend. St. Michael, 'field-marshal and
commander-in-chief of the armies of Heaven', one day met the
Devil, who was playing with a huge block of granite which he
had brought from the mouth of Hell and which, naturally, was
called Hell's Stone. A fight ensued, and the saint won. The
Devil flew away in a panic and dropped the stone into the yard
of the *Angel Inn*, where it remained until 1783. Eventually
Hell's Stone became Helston. A more prosaic and doubtless
accurate explanation is given in the *Oxford Dictionary of Place
Names*. Helston is derived from Henlistone; the Cornish 'hen'
means 'old', and 'lis' was a court or hall. The town was once
called the Old Court Town.

Furry Day is a general holiday in Helston, and in former
times anyone found working was compelled to pay a fine or
make an impossible leap across a wide part of the river. Early
in the morning children and young people go into the countryside to collect flowers, leaves and branches of hawthorn. They
return to the town with their trophies, thus 'fetching the
summer home'. The first dance is at 7 a.m. (once the servants'
dance), and the children's dance starts at 10 a.m. The midday
dance is performed by prominent citizens, the women in summer

dresses, and the men in formal morning suits, all with lily-of-the-valley buttonholes. Between the first two dances the Hal-an-Tow, a sort of folk play, is performed, during which the Hal-an-Tow song is sung. This part of the ceremony is much older than the dance itself. The words of the song make reference to Robin Hood, St. George, the Spaniards and Aunt Mary Moses, the man-woman of the mummer's play, who was once part of the dance.

> *Robin Hood and Little John,*
> *They both are gone to the fair, O;*
> *And we to the merry greenwood,*
> *To see what they do there, O.*
> *And for to chase, O,*
> *To chase the buck and doe,*
> *With Hal-an-Tow,*
> *Jolly rumble, O.*
>
> *And we were up as soon as any day, O,*
> *And for to fetch the summer home,*
> *The summer and the May, O,*
> *For summer is a-come, O,*
> *And winter is a-go, O,*
> *With Hal-an-Tow,*
> *Jolly rumble, O.*

The dancers, traditionally led by a Helston-born couple, advance along the narrow streets as they execute the simple steps to the Furry Dance tune, played by the Town Band. Their circuitous route leads them through the front doors of houses and out of the back doors, which are left open so that the occupants can be brought the luck of summer.

Furry Day festivities end with a ball in the evening. During the day the booths and sideshows of a fair can be found in a field below the town, and stalls line the main street.

Early this century a singer called Katie Moss featured the Furry Dance in a ballad she composed and called *The Floral Dance*, and it has been a popular drawing-room offering of baritones ever since.

May 13th   Abbotsbury,
Garland Day   Dorset

Abbotsbury Garland Day was once connected with blessing the fishing boats at the opening of the mackerel fishing season, and is supposed to have a thousand years' history. This is more than likely for there is a strong hint of pagan sacrifice about the proceedings. Nowadays the custom is kept alive by children. They parade round the village of stone-built thatched cottages with flower garlands on poles and call at all the houses, collecting a fee for showing their handiwork. The flowers are afterwards placed on the War Memorial in the churchyard.

Before the decline of the fishing industry in Abbotsbury, the ceremony had a more satisfying climax. After the villagers had been visited the children took their garlands to the church, where a special service was held—another example of the Church appropriating rites which were originally designed to appease pre-Christian gods. In the evening the procession went down to the beach and the flowers were put in the fishing boats and taken out to sea. They were cast on the water with a prayer and a hymn, and the fishing season was duly open. When there were no more boats going out from Abbotsbury there was naturally little point in continuing that part of the rites, but 'Would you like to see my garland?' is a contemporary reminder of the ancient luck-bringing ceremony.

May 20th   High Wycombe,
Weighing the Mayor   Buckinghamshire

This ancient and inexplicable tradition, which has no connection with May Day, is followed with much ceremony at the annual mayoral installation. Outside the Town Hall in the early evening, after the election, a policeman or other official solemnly weighs the Mayor, Mayoress, Recorder, Town Clerk and Aldermen. The beadle rings his bell and, to the cheers and jeers of the crowd, announces the weights of the dignitaries and by how much they differ from their weights of the previous year.

May 23rd   Rye,
Mayoring Day   Sussex

Rye, once an important port but now an inland town, has a

custom which is a reminder of the days when the town had the privilege of minting its own coins. About noon on Mayoring Day, the Mayor in his robes and chain of office, his Aldermen and Councillors throw hot pennies from the windows of the Mayor's Parlour or from the balcony of the *George Hotel*. Grown-ups, who used to participate in the ceremony, now stand back and let the children waiting in the street below scramble for the coins.

May 25th   Ickwell,
Maypole Dancing   Bedfordshire

The village of Ickwell has a fine maypole, and though May Day festivities are late in the month they are enthusiastically carried out, with dancing round the maypole and the crowning of the May Queen. Unusual additions to the ceremony are two 'moggies'—men with black faces who carry brooms as well as collecting-boxes.

May 26th (on or about)   Hastings,
Blessing the Sea   Sussex

Hastings is still a fishing town, in spite of its greater importance as a holiday resort. The local fishing season begins at the end of May, and the custom of blessing the sea goes back to medieval times. It takes place in the evening, starting about 7 p.m., when a procession leaves All Saints' Church and St. Clement's Church, both in the old part of the town. It goes to the fish market, and there the Bishop of the diocese blesses the fishermen and offers prayers for a successful season.

Oak Apple Day

After the restoration of the monarchy on May 29th, 1660, King Charles II entered Whitehall amid great rejoicings by the people of London. The customs attached to May 29th, however, really commemorate the king's adventure in the famous oak tree at Boscobel after the Battle of Worcester in September, 1651, when he successfully hid from his pursuers.

May 29th had had various names: Oak Apple Day, Royal Oak Day, Nettle Day and Shik-Shak Day. Up to the 1920s it was the custom over half the country for young people to wear oak twigs, leaves and 'apples' in their buttonholes and hats, and those who sported such emblems could sting non-wearers with nettles or pelt them with birds' eggs. This privilege, however, only extended until noon.

Sometimes the leaves and 'apples' were gilded. Often ash leaves were substituted for oak in the afternoon. The custom has never completely died out, and in parts of the north of England and the north Midlands it is still unwise for children to forget their old loyalty to the Cavalier cause on May 29th.

In addition to personal emblems, church towers, flagstaffs, porches, doors and windows of houses were decorated, and in Herefordshire horses' harness was interwoven with greenery. Towards the end of the nineteenth century locomotives, engine-sheds and signal-boxes were covered with branches of oak on King Charles's birthday.

May 29th   Royal Hospital,
Founder's Day   Chelsea, London

On May 29th the Chelsea Pensioners celebrate the birthday of Charles II as a reminder that the Royal Hospital was founded by the king for war pensioners. The ceremony has taken place without a break since 1692. There is a parade, inspection, often

by a member of the Royal Family, and a march past. Three cheers for 'King Charles, our pious Founder', are given, followed by three for the reigning sovereign. King Charles's statue in the Figure Court is decorated with oak leaves, which also adorn the scarlet coats of the pensioners. Military bands enliven the proceedings, and there is plum pudding and extra beer for the old men.

May 29th   Castleton, near Tideswell,
Garland Day   Derbyshire

A remarkable Oak Apple Day observance is held in this village in the Peak District. Because of the day, it is generally supposed that it celebrates the restoration of King Charles II to the throne, but that is only half the story. Its origins are much more ancient. It is, in fact, a May King rite which has survived in no other part of the country.

The Garland King and Queen should both be men. The King is dressed in clothes of the Stuart period, with a large bell-shaped garland of flowers on his shoulders. This is topped by a posy, called the 'queen'. The Queen is heavily veiled. Early in the evening of May 29th the King and Queen are led through the streets on horseback, accompanied by the Town Band and a team of Morris dancers. The procession makes its way to the market-place and the 'queen' from the top of the garland is placed on the War Memorial. The rest of the garland is hoisted to a pinnacle on the church tower by six men, and remains there for a week.

May 29th   Wishford Magna,
Grovely Forest Rights Procession   Wiltshire

On May 29th the villagers of Wishford Magna take part in a curious symbolic ceremony. It has nothing to do with Charles II, but concerns the preservation of the rights of the village people to gather dry wood from Grovely Forest, granted by a Royal Charter in the early seventeenth century. On this day only they are permitted to go to the forest and cut down the largest branch of green wood they can carry, 'by strength of people' and not by mechanical means.

Jack-in-the-Green representing Spring in a May Day procession

Plate 1

Maypole Procession at Thaxted, Essex

(*above*) Sword dance at Flamborough, Yorkshire

Plate 2

(*left*) The unicorn of the Westminster Morris Men at Thaxted, Essex

Hobby-horse Festival at Padstow, Cornwall

Plate 3

Hobby-horse Festival, Minehead, Somerset

Plate 4

(*below*) Oak Apple Day, Wishford Magna, Dorset

The wood is cut early in the morning. At midday a procession, starting from a tree at the south end of the village, marches up the village, headed by a man carrying a banner bearing the words: 'Grovely! Grovely! Grovely! And all Grovely! Unity is Strength!'

The air quivers with the sound of drums and bugles. A flag and mace-bearer precede the banner, and behind it walk four women with bundles of sticks on their heads. Children in fancy dress and men carrying oak boughs follow, and when the cut branches have been collected from the forest they are laid before the village houses.

Before the village cremonies a party goes by bus to Salisbury Cathedral and an offering of boughs is laid before the High Altar. The rest of the day is given up to sports and other festivities.

Ascension Eve   Boyes Staith, Whitby,
Planting the Penny Hedge   Yorkshire

The Penny (Penance) Hedge is a fence made of stakes interleaved with boughs, which is set up at the water's edge at Boyes Staith. It is essential that the Hedge must be strong enough to withstand the force of three tides.

The story of the Penny Hedge starts in 1159, when three hunters were chasing a wild boar. The animal sought refuge in the cell of a hermit in a wood called Eskdale Side, near Whitby. The hermit closed the cell door to keep out the hounds, but the hunters broke in and began to belabour him with their staves.

The Abbot of Whitby arrived on the scene just before the hermit died. He was prepared to punish the hunters severely, but was persuaded not to do so by the dying holy man. As a penance for their cruelty the hunters, and their descendants, had to cut stakes from Stray-head Wood once a year and plant them at the water's edge in Whitby Harbour. While they were cutting the stakes and making the hedge the Abbot's bailiff was to sound his horn, read out the details of their crime, and then cry out, 'Out upon you!'

This picturesque story was probably made up to fit a custom already being observed for which there seemed to be no explanation, but which was likely to have been originally a condition of land tenure in Saxon times.

The people who perform the ceremony nowadays are not necessarily descendants of the three murderers. The crime is not recited, but the ancient cry is heard. The ceremony is attended by Church and civic dignitaries, and is watched by townspeople and visitors.

Ascension Day   Tissington,
Well-dressing   Derbyshire

Well-dressing, the custom of decorating wells with elaborate floral religious pictures, is a survival of a very ancient belief that water was the dwelling-place of spirits that had to be appeased by sacrificial rites. Water gods were common in the Middle East; the rivers Euphrates, Nile and Ganges each had its own, and the Jews regarded Jordan and the pools of Siloam and Bethesda as sacred because of their healing properties. In the early days of Britain the gods of the Tweed, Spey and Dart were said to demand a human sacrifice every year.

In ancient Rome flowers were thrown into decorated wells at the Festival of Fontinalia to keep the nymphs of wells and fountains happy. When Christianity superseded the pagan gods, holy wells were given the names of saints or the Madonna, and baptismal services were held by the well. But in spite of the Church's efforts, the cult of water-worship remained deeply rooted and widespread, and a belief that well water can cure sickness still persists.

Well-dressing ceremonies were common in several English counties, especially in Staffordshire, Shropshire and Derbyshire. Tissington in Derbyshire, where there are five wells, is probably the best known place. According to local belief, the festival was first held in 1350, after the Black Death had abated. While the plague raged and half the population of Derbyshire died, the people of Tissington survived because the well water remained uncontaminated. In the early seventeenth century, when there was a severe drought, Tissington's wells continued to provide an adequate supply of pure water.

The wells are decorated with flowers and garlands in various designs, from Biblical scenes to the portrayal of contemporary events. Frames and figures of wood are covered with clay and moss, and upon the surface flower petals, leaves, buds and berries are arranged to form coloured characters, mosaic work and texts. The result is often a beautiful work of art that is admired by thousands of visitors.

Each well is dressed by its own team of village people, and preparations begin weeks beforehand. A celebration service is held in the church on Ascension Day, the Thursday before Whitsuntide. After this, a procession, headed by the local clergy, choir and congregation, visits each well in turn, and the water is blessed in gratitude for past favours.

Throughout the summer, until the end of August, dressed wells can be seen at other places in Derbyshire: Wirksworth (Whit Saturday), Youlgreave (the Saturday nearest June 24th), Stoney Middleton (the Saturday before the old August Bank Holiday), Barlow (the Wednesday after August 10th), Eyam (the last week in August), and Buxton (the Thursday nearest June 24th). At Hope and Tideswell the date is usually the last Saturday in June.

Whitsuntide

WHITSUNTIDE comes seven weeks after Easter. It is the third of the Church's great festivals, and the least understood. Birth, death and resurrection are comparatively simple concepts, but the descent of 'tongues of fire' and the gift of a comforting spirit is less easy for human minds to assimilate. Christmas celebrations became wedded to the primitive rejoicings in the sun's birth; Easter was foreshadowed by rites connected with the rebirth of the slain god; but there is nothing in pagan ritual that corresponds to Whitsuntide. It occurs too early for midsummer, and so has to make do with what is left over from Easter and May Day. Thus we find the decoration of churches, Morris and maypole dancing, and the presence of a Lord and Lady in the revels.

The main feature of Whitsuntide used to be the Whitsun Church Ale, a parish feast akin to the *Agapae*, the love-feasts of the early Church, when congregations met and feasted after they had received Communion together; those who were rich brought enough for themselves and the poor, and all ate together for the increase of mutual love.

The Whitsun Ales were encouraged by the first Stuart kings. After the feast there were games and sports, Morris dancing and drinking. Parsons approved of such activities only if they did not interfere with attendance at church. The profits from the feast, which might be anything between five and twenty pounds, went towards the upkeep of the church or were given to the poor, for whom there was often no other kind of Public Assistance. John Aubrey describes a Whitsun Ale, but his words are far too sober for what must have been something of an un-sober occasion. 'In every parish was a church-house,' he says, 'to which belonged spits, crocks, and other utensils for dressing provisions. Here the housekeepers met. The young people were there too, and had dancing, bowling, shooting at butts, etc., the ancients sitting gravely by, and looking on.'

A Lord and Lady of the Ale, synonymous with the King and Queen of the May, were elected every year and became the presiding officers; they were attended by a mace-bearer and a Fool. Many churchwardens' accounts give interesting details of the appointments of the Lord and Lady, the expenses incurred, and the profits made on the amusements and the ale itself. In 1621 the Chapel of St. Lawrence, Brentford, paid the Lady five shillings. In 1624 the chapel made £4 19s. at bagatelle, £2 by raffling, and £8 on the sale of ale.

In the nineteenth century Whitsun Ale observances had diminished into Club Feasts and Club Walks, though few of these rural clubs, with their background of charitable works, have survived into modern times. The usual order of proceedings was a church service, then a procession, ending with Morris dancing and games. The north of England, however, particularly Lancashire and Yorkshire, still sees Walking Days, which are organised by the churches for Sunday and Day School children. In the larger towns such as Manchester and Warrington shops close, traffic is diverted, and the streets are lined with spectators. The children follow a traditional route and walk behind banners. They are dressed in white, the girls veiled and wreathed, carrying bunches of flowers. Older people follow, some of them proud to be walking for the fiftieth time. In many villages and towns in Cornwall the procession follows a brass band and the whole place is given over to holiday-makers.

From the early part of the twelfth century performances of Miracle and Mystery Plays were very popular at Whitsuntide, especially in the time of Chaucer. Each city and town guild chose its own play, and together they presented a series. The

Mystery Plays were on subjects taken from the New Testament on the life of Christ; the Miracle Plays dealt with other parts of Scripture or with the life of a saint.

The most famous Whitsuntide Miracle Plays took place in Chester, where, in 1600, twenty-five guilds covered the whole story of salvation from the Creation of the World to the Last Judgement. The Tanners were responsible for the Fall of Lucifer; the Drapers for the Creation and the pageant of Adam and Eve; the Water-carriers took on the Deluge, the Barbers Abraham and Isaac; the Wrighters performed the Nativity, the

Bakers the Passion; and the Skinners played Christ appearing to the two Disciples. The Christian story may have been sometimes distorted, but the person of Christ was always sacred. Devils tended to be humorous characters, Herod was a burlesque figure, and farce intruded in unexpected places. The complete cycle of plays reads, and must have acted, powerfully and with vivid realism. They were presented on a stage like a high double-decker cart which could be wheeled from one part of the town to another. The upper deck formed the stage, the lower one the actors' dressing-room.

Miracle Plays are by no means obsolete, and some of the

Chester, York and Coventry cycles are quite often performed at festivals of various kinds. Two of the Chester cycle in particular have achieved popularity through being set to music by Benjamin Britten. His *Second Canticle* is a setting of Abraham and Isaac; and *Noye's Fludde* takes the form of an opera performed mainly by children.

The revival of Morris dancing reaches its annual peak at Whitsuntide. Thaxted, a small Essex town with a beautiful church and a magnificent fifteenth-century Guild Hall, is noted for Whitsuntide dancing, though it also takes place there at Easter, on Trinity Sunday, Boxing Day, and in June. From the church the dancers tour the streets, passing the Guild Hall and the Recorder's House en route.

At Bampton, in Oxfordshire, the dancing starts early in the morning on Whit Monday, and goes on all day. The ritual cake, stuck on a decorated sword, accompanies the dancers.

Back in the sixteenth century, Philip Stubbes had as little use for Morris dancers as he had for the maypole. He describes their antics scathingly and with probably more than a little exaggeration: 'They bedeck themselves with scarves, ribbons and laces hanged all over with gold rings, precious stones, and other jewels; this done, they tie about either leg twenty or forty bells, with rich handkerchiefs in their hands, and sometimes laid across their shoulders and necks, borrowed for the most part of their pretty Mopsies and loving Bessies, for bussing them in the dark. Thus all things set in order, then have they their hobby-horses, dragons and other antics, together with their gaudy pipers and thundering drummers to strike up the devil's dance withal. Then march these heathen company towards the church and churchyard, their pipers piping, their drummers thundering, their stumps dancing, their bells jingling, their handkerchiefs swinging about their heads like madmen, their hobby-horses and other monsters skirmishing among the throng; and in this sort they go to the church (I say) and into the church, (though the minister be at prayer or preaching), dancing and swinging their handkerchiefs, over their heads in the church, like devils incarnate, with such a confused noise, that no man can hear his own voice.'

Whit Sunday   St. Briavels,
Bread and Cheese Dole   Gloucestershire

St. Briavels is a small village in the Forest of Dean. After the
church service on Whit Sunday baskets of bread and cheese are
taken to a wall, ten feet high, which adjoins the church, and a
forester throws small pieces to the congregation leaving the
church. The scramble ends when the forester holds the basket
upside down to show that it is empty. This custom is said to
date from 1206 and to be connected with conditions of land
tenure. King John granted to the villagers of St. Briavels and
Havelsfield the rights of cutting and taking away timber from
certain lands and of retaining grazing rights. In medieval times
the bread and cheese was given to the poor of the village; each
householder had to pay twopence towards the cost.

Whit Monday   Kingsteignton,
Ram Fair   Devon

This is a Whitsuntide activity which provides a direct link
with pre-Christian animal rites. The carcase of a young ram,
decked with ribbons and flowers, is paraded through the town.
Later, during the games and dancing which follow, it is roasted,
cut up, and the pieces are sold. The legend attached to the
ceremony relates how the stream which supplied the village
with water suddenly dried up, and the priests advised that
prayers to the gods should be offered. The prayers were
miraculously answered by the appearance of a new spring
which rose in a water meadow, and a ram was then ritually
burned as a thank-offering. The spring was called Fair Water
and never ran dry. Formerly a live lamb was taken round the
streets on Whit Monday in a cart adorned with lilac and
laburnum, and the onlookers were expected to contribute
towards the expenses of the ceremony.

Whit Monday   Cooper's Hill,
Cheese-rolling   Birdlip, Gloucestershire

The custom of cheese-rolling is at least four hundred years
old, and is intended to remind the villagers of their rights to
graze their sheep on the hill, which has a gradient of one in

three. In the early evening of Whit Monday, the Master of Ceremonies, dressed in an ancient smock and wearing a be-ribboned top hat, bowls the cheese, which is tied up with ribbons, down the hill. It is pursued by boys and young men, and the one who captures it is allowed to keep the cheese and also gets a small prize. The starting point of the chase is marked by a flagstaff, which is a reminder that the custom also celebrates the rights of the people to dance round the maypole.

Whit Monday   Dunmow,
Dunmow Flitch Trial   Essex

The award of a flitch of bacon to any couple who can prove that they have not quarrelled or regretted their marriage for a year and a day has a history going back at least to the thirteenth century, when Robert Fitzwalter instituted the ceremony in the reign of Henry III. Chaucer refers to the flitch, and so does William Langland in *Piers Plowman*. 'For since the Plague hundreds of couples have married, yet the only fruit they have brought forth are foul words: they live in jealousy, without happiness, and lie in bed quarrelling, so that all the children they get are strife and nagging! If they went to try for the Dunmow Flitch, they wouldn't stand a chance without the Devil's help; and unless they were both lying there'd be no bacon for them.'

Claimants for the Dunmow Flitch are required to answer questions about their marriage at a mock trial, presided over by a judge. They are represented by 'counsel', and a jury consisting of six maidens and six bachelors gives the verdict. In its early days the trial was conducted by the Prior of Little Dunmow Priory, which was founded in 1104.

The first recorded award was made in 1445, and old records contain details of many subsequent awards. The custom was not always observed annually and was frequently allowed to lapse. In 1772 the Lord of the Manor stopped the presentation. Later it was revived but was abolished as a 'nuisance' in 1809. The subsequent revival as a regular event was largely due to the novelist Harrison Ainsworth who, in 1855, presented the prize. One of his novels, *The Flitch of Bacon*, concerns the much-married landlord of the *Dunmow Flitch Inn* and his attempts to win the bacon.

Until the eighteenth century, application for the flitch was a man's prerogative, the implication being that a happy marriage was one that was satisfactory only to the husband. Winners of the flitch were once carried through the streets in the Prior's chair, which is now kept in Little Dunmow church. Although capacious, the chair was hardly big enough for two people, except such as had already given ample proof of their mutual regard. In its early days the trial was treated much more seriously than it is today, and winners were few and far between. In fact, when the flitch was first awarded, the only successful claimants were a sea-captain and his wife who had not seen each other from their wedding day until the day of the ceremony. A nineteenth-century claimant was a Yeoman of the Royal Body-guard, over sixty years of age, and the bravery which had carried him through the Crimean War and the Indian Mutiny no doubt helped him to face the 'trial'.

Whit Monday   St. Ives,
Dicing for Bibles   Huntingdonshire

This incongruous custom started in 1675 when Dr. Robert Wilde bequeathed £50 to provide the poor children of the parish with Bibles. He made the condition that they had to be diced for in church, and until the church was damaged in 1918 that is where the ceremony took place. Up to 1880 the altar was used as a gaming-table, but the Bishop then decided that a more suitable place should be found, and a table by the chancel steps was used instead. Nowadays the dicing takes place in the nearby Church School.

Six Bibles are disposed of in this way every year, and twelve children, six belonging to the Church of England, and six Nonconformists, cast lots for them. The vicar superintends the proceedings.

Whit Monday   Lichfield,
Court of Arraye and Greenhill Bower   Staffordshire

This very ancient custom probably dates from the twelfth century. The people of Lichfield, which at that time was a small but growing town built round the Norman cathedral, had to provide a certain amount of armour each year for the defence of the cathedral walls. The armour was inspected by the Court of Arraye of Men and Arms on Bower Hill. In return for their contribution the citizens were granted trading privileges.

Nowadays young men, wearing coats of mail, parade before the Court officials. There is also a procession of flowers, which commemorates a medieval pleasure fair called Greenhill Bower.

Whit Monday   Laugharne,
Common Walk   Carmarthenshire, Wales

A Common Walk was held in 1969, and succeeding ones will be at three-yearly intervals. The reason for the custom is to 'beat the bounds' and preserve the people's common rights and privileges, which were first granted under a fourteenth-century charter.

At 5 a.m. the Bailiff rings the Town Hall bell. The Portreeve (Mayor) leads the procession, and he is followed by halberd-men, the Common Attorney and the Grand Jury. The course is twenty-four miles long, and halts are made at 'hoisting' places, where the bounds are beaten and refreshments taken.

Saturday after Whitsun
Scuttlebrook Wake (Cotswold Games)　　　Chipping Campden,
　　　　　　　　　　　　　　　　　　　　　　　Gloucestershire

The famous Cotswold Games were revived for the Festival of Britain celebrations in 1951 after a lapse of a hundred years. They were held on Dover's Hill, between Chipping Campden and Weston-sub-Edge, from which there is a magnificent view of the Vale of Evesham and far beyond.

Robert Dover, a Warwickshire lawyer, was a vigorous opponent of Puritanism, and in 1605 he obtained permission from James I to hold an annual event for the 'harmless mirths and jollitie' of the people of the neighbourhood. The Games were held on Dover's Hill until 1851. They included cudgelling, wrestling, skittles, football, hare-hunting and cock-fighting. In 1819 horse-racing was added. In the nineteenth century hooliganism increased to such an extent that the Games were abandoned.

Scuttlebrook Wake is organised on more modest lines. The Scuttlebrook Queen is crowned at a point where the Scuttlebrook stream once flowed into the High Street. There is a fancy dress competition, folk dancing, and races and competitions for the children.

(Since the change to Spring Bank Holiday, all 'Whit Monday' events now take place on the last Monday in May.)

June to August

Thursday of the week June 6th–12th   Lanark,
Lanimer Day   Lanarkshire, Scotland

Lanimer (or Land March) Day is when the boundary stones which mark out the land that King David I of Scotland gave to the citizens of Lanark in the twelfth century are inspected. The Land March is also called 'The Birks' because birch branches are carried in the procession. The whole town is decorated. The parade is led by the civic authorities, accompanied by bands, and is dominated by a series of tableaux. The Lanimer Queen and her maids of honour ride in the procession. Later she is crowned.

A second procession starts at noon. This one is led by the Lord Cornet (a standard-bearer) on horseback, who is chosen annually by the Town Council. The riding of the marches is interrupted by a visit to the Moor for sports and horse races. At the end of the day the Town Clerk announces that the boundaries are still intact. During the ceremony a silver bell, nearly 900 years old, is struck.

Thursday of the first full week in June
Riding the Marches

Hawick, Roxburghshire and Selkirk, Selkirkshire, Scotland

In these two towns, twelve miles apart, the colourful ceremony goes back to late medieval times, when border warfare between England and Scotland was rife, and particularly to the Battle of Flodden in 1513, when the Scots were utterly defeated.

In the following year the young men of Hawick, the Callans, captured an English banner after defeating the company holding it, and this event, coming so soon after the disaster of Flodden, has been celebrated every year since, between June 5th and 11th. On the Thursday evening the Cornet, who has been elected in May, is presented with a copy of the flag (a gold diagonal cross on a blue ground) which was captured from the English. It is decorated with ribbons and figures in all the processions.

Riding the Marches begins early the next day. After various ceremonies, the Cornet leads the procession on horseback, carrying the flag. After he has ridden round the race-course, the staff of the flag is lowered into the Coble Pool to mark one of the old boundaries. Later it is flown from a window of the Council Chamber. In the evening the Cornet's Ball is held, at which *Teribus*, the Common Riding song, is sung, and the Cornet's Reel is danced. Racing, athletics, band performances and social events are held throughout the period.

At Selkirk the festival of Common Riding is also associated with the Battle of Flodden. Tradition says that only one soldier from Selkirk returned alive to the town, and he bore a captured English flag. The standard-bearer now leads about 200 riders, each with a flag, in procession round the town boundaries. When they return to the market-place the flags are waved backwards, forwards and round the head to the tune of *Up wi' the Souters o' Selkirk*.

Common Riding can also be found in June at Galashiels, Linlithgow, Duns, Langholm and Lauder.

June (during first week)   Bideford,
Beating the Clock Race   Devon

This unusual foot race has been held for the last fifty or so years. The River Torridge is spanned by a bridge with twenty-four arches. The parish clock takes twenty-one and four-fifths seconds to strike eight, and the aim of those who take part in the race is to cross the bridge before the eighth stroke sounds.

June 20th (on or near)   Abingdon,
Electing the Mayor of Ock Street   Berkshire

During the eighteenth century it was the custom for a black ox to be roasted at Abingdon, near Oxford. This took place on or near the Feast of St. Edmund of Abingdon, which is June 19th, the day before St. Edmund's Fair. The meat was given to the poor people of the town.

In the year 1700, according to one story (1752, according to another), there was a fight between two factions, the up-town men and the down-town men, following an argument about who should have the head, horns and tail of the ox. An imaginary line was drawn through the town, and Ock Street (which is named after the River Ock) divided the party of the east from the party of the north. The fight was long and exhausting. It was eventually won by the east party when a man named Hemmings, one of Abingdon's Morris dancers, captured the horns. He was proclaimed 'Mayor of Ock Street'.

A Mayor of Ock Street is still elected annually, but not nowadays after a fight. Instead, there is an election. The inhabitants of Ock Street, where the candidate must have been born, place their ballot papers into a box and the votes are counted openly before the candidates. The winner, usually a member of the Hemmings family, which has been connected with the event since its beginning, celebrates his victory by drinking from the 'mace', which is a wooden bowl with a silver rim, thought to be over two hundred years old. He is carried in triumphal procession through the streets by the Abingdon Morris dancers, led by the hornbearer, who carries the ancient horns of the black ox mounted on a wooden head on top of a pole. The date '1700' is painted on the pole.

Morris dancing begins in the early evening outside an inn called the *Ock Street Horns*. The dancers, who wear top hats, white shirts, and trousers decorated with bells and ribbons, visit all the inns in Ock Street and the market-place, finishing up in the courtyard of the *Crown and Thistle*. The mace is refilled at each inn, for dancing is thirsty work. A Fool accompanies the dancers, and he hits out indiscriminately with a bladder tied to an ox's tail.

The 'Mayor', of course, has no other function than to lead the dancers, but the real Mayor of Abingdon honours the proceedings by a ceremonial visit.

Mid-June   Peebles,
Beltane Festival   Peeblesshire, Scotland

Beltane was an important Celtic fire festival celebrated on May 1st. A charter for a fair to be held on Beltane Day was granted to the people of Peebles by James VI, and this is combined with the annual March Riding, though transferred from May to June; and a week of picturesque pageantry ensues.

When the Beltane Fair has been declared open the Beltane Queen is crowned on the steps of the old parish church. In 1922 the Coronation Chair was provided by ex-Peebleans living in South Africa, and in 1925 expatriates in Canada presented the town with a silver casket which contains a scroll bearing the names of the Beltane Queens. New Zealand ex-Peebleans gave the magnificent Coronation robes in the same year. Peebles already owned the Beltane Bell (a fourteenth century horse-racing trophy). The present bell is made from silver, and is a copy of the Liberty Bell in Philadelphia. It was presented by ex-Peebleans living in America.

The Riding of the Marches includes a circuit of the town boundaries by the Cornet and his supporters, and the Colours are 'bussed' by the Cornet's Lass.

June 23rd (Midsummer Eve)   Stonehenge,
Druids' Ceremony   Salisbury Plain, Wiltshire

The members of the Church of the Druid Universal Bond perform their annual rites at dawn on Midsummer Day to honour the Summer Solstice, which is actually June 21st. A vigil is kept through the night, and when the first rays of the rising sun shine on the 'Altar Stone' the dawn service begins. The Chief Druid leads a white-robed, scarlet-hooded procession round the circle of stones and halts at the Altar Stone. Another service is held at midday.

The theory that Stonehenge was a temple built by the Druids before the Roman occupation of Britain has been completely

The children's dance on Furry Day at Helston, Cornwall

Plate 5

(*right*) Garland Day at Castleton, Derbyshire. Framework of the garland

Plate 6

(*right*) Covering the framework

(*left*) The completed garland

(*above*) Well-dressing at Tissington, Derbyshire

Plate 7

(*left*) Well-dressing at Wirksworth, Derbyshire

Morris dancing at Bampton, Oxfordshire

Plate 8

Morris dancing at Headington, Oxfordshire

exploded. Stonehenge was probably started in the Early Bronze Age, nearly 4,000 years ago, and there were at least three building periods. It is likely that the site was taken over by Druidic priests in the Iron Age as a temple for sacrificial rites, but the modern Order of Druids, which claims to be a survival of the ancient priests of Britain, has no such bloodthirsty leanings. Today's ceremony is a milk-and-water, faintly comic spectacle which attracts the crowds and brings out the television cameras, but which occasions no superstitious terror.

June 23rd St. Cleer,
Banishing the Witches near Liskeard, Cornwall

Cornwall is a county where belief in fairies, evil spirits and witches has always been strong, and even today Cornish people have not completely shaken off their fears.

One of the most propitious times for combatting the forces of evil was Midsummer Eve, and relics of former practices can still be found. At St. Cleer a huge bonfire, crowned with a witch's broom and hat, is lit on a hill, as a warning to witches to steer clear of that area for a year. In order to break any spell that a witch may have cast, forty varieties of herbs and flowers are cast into the flames. A wooden sickle, cut from an oak tree, is also thrown on the fire, probably as a symbol of the human sacrifice that was offered in pagan times.

June 23rd
St. John's Eve Midsummer Bonfires   Cornwall

The old pagan custom of lighting a chain of bonfires on St.
John's Eve was revived in Cornwall in the 1920s. The custom
originated in the attempt to boost the power of the sun, the
source of life and fire, which, after Midsummer Day, slowly
begins to ebb.

The first bonfire is lit at St. Ives, and all through the night
the fires blaze across the whole county, from west to east.
Before each fire is lit the Master of Ceremonies gives a blessing
in the old Cornish language. A girl chosen as Lady of the
Flowers throws a sickle-shaped bunch of flowers and herbs into
the flames with an appropriate invocation. Sometimes young
couples, hand in hand, will jump through the flames to bring
themselves good luck. When the fires have burned out the
ashes are kept to form the foundation of the beacon that will be
lit the following year.

June 28th   Warrington,
Warrington Walking Day   Lancashire

Thousands of children from churches and schools of all
denominations walk in procession through the main streets of
the town—a custom started by the Rector of Warrington in
1835. His aim was to draw attention to the fact that the
Newtown and Latchford Heath Races, which were held on
June 28th, caused much hardship and distress to the children of
those parents who lost their money on the horses. The races
are no more, but the Walk continues, and the day is a public
holiday.

The children first meet before the Town Hall. Then, led by
bands and banners, they march past the Mayor and Town
Council and process through the streets, which are closed to
traffic. They return to their churches and chapels for a short
service, and in the afternoon play games or visit the seaside.

Walking Days are a characteristically northern custom,
strong in Yorkshire and Lancashire. Those held at Manchester
and Salford are especially noteworthy, for the routes cover
several miles.

June 30th   Galashiels,
Braw Lads' Gathering   Selkirkshire, Scotland

The Gathering was instituted as recently as 1930, but it is a revival of the old Riding the Marches ceremony. Each of the five wards of the town elect a Braw (handsome) Lad and Lass, and from the five couples the chief Braw Lad and Lass are chosen. The other four couples act as attendants.

In the morning of the great day the Provost of the city presents the Burgh Flag to the Braw Lad. He, mounted on horseback and accompanied by scores of mounted followers, rides the marches, taking the traditional route which includes Abbotsford, the home of Sir Walter Scott. Included in the day's pageantry is the 'Sour Plums Raid', which takes place at the Englishman's Dyke. This commemorates an event of 1337, when the men of Galashiels came upon a band of English raiders eating the fruit of the wild plum trees. The surprised Englishmen were soon routed, and the little local victory gave rise to a popular song called *Sour Plums*. The phrase was adopted as the town's motto, and has remained so to this day.

Another part of the ceremony takes place at the Old Town Cross to mark the marriage of James IV of Scotland to Margaret Tudor which, a century later, led to the Union of Scotland and England. Braw Lads' Gathering ends, after a day of sports, civic entertainment and a fancy dress ball, at the War Memorial. There the Braw Lass places bunches of roses and thistles at the foot of the Church Cross.

July 4th   Whalton,
Baal Fire   Northumberland

July 4th is Old Midsummer Eve, and a ceremonial bonfire is lit on the village green as darkness falls. The village children dance round it in a ring; later the grown-ups dance to the music of a fiddle, and there is a distribution of sweets, for which the children scramble.

July 5th   St. John's,
Tynwald Ceremony   Isle of Man

At St. John's is Tynwald Hill, which is reputed to be made of the soil of the seventeen ancient parishes of the island. It is about twelve feet high, eighty-five feet in diameter at the base, and has four circular platforms at three-foot intervals.

On July 5th, Old Midsummer Day, the Lieutenant-Governor of the Isle of Man, who represents the reigning monarch, leaves St. John's Chapel after a service and, attended by officials of the State and Church, follows his Swordbearer through lines of guards to Tynwald Hill. He sits on a crimson velvet chair on the top platform, facing the east, and the Sword of State, which

dates from the thirteenth century, is laid before him. Beside him the Deemsters, or Judges, take their places, together with members of the Legislative Council, and behind them stand the twenty-four members of the House of Keys, the world's smallest Parliament. Behind them are the clergy and members of the Bar, and the lowest platform is occupied by minor officials. All present wear a sprig of St. John's Wort to mark St. John's Day.

The ceremony begins after the Court has been 'fenced'—that is, warned not to quarrel or brawl. At one time the mound was actually roped off from the spectators, but nowadays the 'fencing' is symbolic only. The Chief Justice reads out the titles of the Acts of Parliament which have been passed at Westminster during the year, first in English, then in Manx, the old language of the island. This formality indicates that the English Acts are accepted by the Isle of Man and become law there. Apart from foreign policy, defence and currency, the legislature of the Isle of Man has complete control over the island's affairs.

'Tynwald' is derived from the Norse 'Thing vollr', which means a fenced open Parliament, and the ceremony has associations with the time when the island was the property of the Vikings. Records of the Tynwald Ceremony go back to the thirteenth century, but it is probably at least three hundred years older. Until 1752 it was held on Midsummer Day, June 24th, but the islanders rejected the alteration in the calendar and kept to July 5th.

July 8th   South Queensferry,
The Burry Man   West Lothian, Scotland

On the day before Ferry Fair, a strange custom is observed, the origins of which are shrouded in mystery. This is the appearance of the Burry Man in the streets of South Queensferry, west of Edinburgh on the Firth of Forth. The fantastically dressed figure has been seen on this day for over 600 years. He is covered from head to foot in a close-fitting garment covered with thistle and teazle burrs, and his head-dress, made of flowers, conceals all his features. It is traditional that nobody should recognise the Burry Man.

He carries a staff in each hand, and he goes through the streets speaking to no one. He is greeted with respect at every house he visits, and often receives money to bring good luck to the householders.

It is possible that the annual appearance of the Burry Man commemorates an actual historical event, for it is said that King Malcolm III of Scotland escaped from the English by covering himself with burrs and flowers. Another explanation links the Burry Man with the old custom of collecting market or fair tolls.

July 11th   Appleton,
Bawming the Thorn   Cheshire

Bawming (adorning or anointing) the Thorn is one of
England's oldest customs. It is in fact part of May Day celebrations, the difference at Appleton being that dancing takes place,
not round a maypole but round a living hawthorn tree that has
been decorated with flowers. Tradition has it that the tree has
grown from a cutting of the original Holy Thorn at Glastonbury, but the present tree is only about seventy years old.

The day starts with a procession through the streets of the
village. Children, themselves garlanded, carry their tributes of
flowers and ribbons to the tree and 'bawm' both it and the iron
railings which protect it. Then they dance round it.

Tree worship is of great antiquity. Our ancestors believed
that a tree could contain a god which would protect the village,
and a single tree in a central position was particularly revered.
In early times the village council would meet under such a tree
to dispense justice.

July 12th   Belfast,
Battle of the Boyne Celebrations   Northern Ireland

After James II had abdicated in 1688 he fled to France, but a
few months later, making his final bid for the throne of England,
he invaded Ireland and, with the help of the Irish Guards,
appeared to be in sight of victory. The Earl of Tyrconnell had
captured nearly all the Protestant strongholds in the north;
only Derry and Enniskillen had refused to capitulate.

On July 1st, 1690, William of Orange (William III of
England), with an army of 30,000 men, defeated James's army
of 25,000 French and Irish troops at the line of the River Boyne.
On July 12th, 1691, a more decisive battle was fought at
Aughrim, during which the French general was killed and his
army put to rout.

The two battles are commemorated on July 12th all over
Ulster, and in the larger towns such as Belfast, Londonderry
and Omagh there are large-scale celebrations which combine
historical pageants, concerts and carnivals. They are organised
by the Grand Orange Lodges, which are Irish Protestant

organisations dedicated to maintaining Protestant ascendancy wherever possible.

Tuesday and Wednesday after July 19th   Honiton,
Hot Penny Ceremony   Devon

Honiton Fair dates from 1257. It is opened with the old medieval custom of displaying a glove to guarantee that visiting merchants might trade freely at the fair with no fear of arrest or punishment as long as they respected the fair's Charter. Footpads and robbers were in those times a serious threat, and a law passed in the reign of Edward I gave royal protection to law-abiding citizens.

Today the Town Crier carries a gilt glove on top of a decorated staff and proclaims the opening of the fair with a cry of 'Oyez! The glove is up! The fair is open! No man shall be arrested till the glove is taken down! God save the Queen!' Then hot pennies are thrown from the windows of the town's main inns, and children scramble for them.

Displaying a glove is common to several West Country fairs, including those at Exeter, Kingsbridge and Barnstaple.

Rush-bearing

Rush-bearing started as a very practical thing, for it dates back to the times when the floors of churches were made of dry earth or clay, and it was necessary to cover them to lessen the damp and cold. Churchgoers of those times were very hardy people for not even seats were provided until the fifteenth century, and only the wealthy could afford cushions to kneel on. When churches had pews and floors were made of wood or stone, strewing rushes over the floors became unnecessary, but the custom persisted in various forms. It was usually observed on the church's 'wake', the day of dedication. By the beginning of this century only the north of England kept it up. At Ambleside and Grasmere in Westmorland it is still practised.

Up to the end of the nineteenth century the rush-cart was often seen in some northern counties. In south-east Lancashire every village had one, and the rivalry between the villagers was so great that often skulls were cracked and blood was shed during arguments about whose rush-cart was the best.

At rush-bearing time the harvest cart was gaily decorated, piled high with sheaves of rushes, sometimes with a green arbour of branches on top, and men pulled it to the church by flower-covered ropes. Musicians, Morris dancers, a May Queen and a Fool accompanied the cart on its journey.

Saturday nearest July 26th, Feast of St. Anne   Ambleside,
Rush-bearing Festival   Westmorland

St. Anne is the patron saint of Ambleside, a small town at the head of Lake Windermere. Her feast day is now largely a children's day. They carry rushes and flowers woven into patterns and Christian symbols on wooden frames. They go in procession to the market-place, where they sing the *Rush-bearers' Hymn*. This was composed by the Rev. Owen Lloyd, a curate of Ambleside in the early nineteenth century and a friend of William Wordsworth. Then they return to the church for a special service, at the end of which they leave their bearings and receive gingerbread squares.

A similar ceremony is held at Grasmere on the Saturday nearest August 5th, St. Oswald's Day. The clergy and choir, following the saint's banner, lead the procession, then come six girls carrying the 'rush-sheet', which contains flowers and rushes. Other people carry crosses, crowns, harps and triangles, all made of plaited rushes.

The church bells peal as the procession winds its way through the streets to the church, singing *St. Oswald's Hymn* and the *Rush-bearing March*, and the bearings are taken inside. After the service, pieces of gingerbread, on which the saint's name is imprinted, are given out. On the following Monday the bearings are collected by their owners, and a tea and sports bring the festival to an end.

The custom is also observed in the Westmorland village of Warcop on June 29th, St. Peter's Day. There the boys carry rush crosses and the girls wear floral crowns. Crosses and crowns are put round the altar during the service, and afterwards they are hung over the main door of the church, where they remain until St. Peter's Day the following year.

Rush-bearing at St. Mary Redcliffe, in Bristol, takes place on Whit Sunday. In 1493 a Mayor of Bristol left money for a sermon to be preached every year for the incoming Mayor. The custom is still maintained at a service at which the Lord Bishop of the diocese greets the Lord Mayor of Bristol, who is welcomed to the church by the sound of trumpets. The floor of the church is strewn with rushes and the church is decorated with flowers.

First week in August   Meriden,
Great Wardmote of the Woodmen of Arden   Warwickshire
The Great Wardmote is an archery competition which is run on medieval lines. The Forest of Arden once surrounded Meriden, which claims to be the geographical centre of England, and in 1785 the groups of woodmen in the area combined and called themselves the Woodmen of Arden. They wore white trousers, a buff waistcoat, a green coat with silver buttons, and a green hat; and the present-day members of the Society, limited in number to eighty, wear the traditional costume.

They shoot with six-foot yew bows, like those used at Crécy and Agincourt, and their arrows are stamped according to their weight in silver, as they were in medieval times.

The Great Wardmote is held over four days in the first week in August; ordinary wardmotes are held in June and July.

First Saturday in August   Ripon,
Feast of St. Wilfrid   Yorkshire
To commemorate the return from exile of Bishop (later Saint) Wilfrid of York in the seventh century, the people of Ripon hold an annual feast early in August. In the afternoon, 'St. Wilfrid', riding on a white horse, parades through the city to the accompaniment of music from the City Band.

Every night at nine o'clock the custom of Setting the Watch is observed in Ripon. The City Hornblower, wearing a fawn-coloured tunic and tricorne hat, blows a long note on his horn and repeats the performance at each corner of the eighteenth-century obelisk in the market-place. The final blast is given outside the Mayor's house. At the same time the Curfew Bell rings from Ripon Minster.

This ceremony was once the signal for the Wakeman and his assistants to patrol the streets to prevent burglaries. House-holders paid an annual toll for this insurance, and if a burglary was committed after the watch was set, the Wakeman had to pay compensation. The duty of keeping the peace now is the responsibility of the police, but the custom of sounding the horn has never lapsed, so it is said, since 886, during the reign of Alfred the Great. Whether that is true or not, it certainly dates back to medieval times.

A horn used long ago, which may be of Saxon workmanship, is now preserved in the Town Hall. It is attached to a baldric, or belt, of purple velvet, the straps of which are adorned with the silver badges of Ripon's former Wakemen and Mayors. It is brought out only on ceremonial occasions and worn by the Serjeant-at-Mace. The horn now used is nearly a hundred years old, and was made specially for the nightly ceremony.

First week in August
Royal National Eisteddfod of Wales
The site varies between North and South Wales; a different site is chosen every year.

The Royal National Eisteddfod is a competitive song and musical festival for Welsh bards and musicians, and is a great cultural feast. The first Eisteddfod in its modern sense was held in 1451, though events of a similar nature were held hundreds of years before. By the end of the eighteenth century it was firmly established as an annual event, and in roughly the form it takes today.

The aim of the Eisteddfod is to foster Welsh poetry, music, dancing, and arts and crafts. It is conducted solely in Welsh. Each Eisteddfod starts a year and a day before the first event when the Arch Druid, wearing a coronet of oak leaves and a copper breastplate, proclaims the festival from a specially erected stone circle. He also makes the inaugural speech, standing on the Arch Druid's Stone. When he has finished, the Sword of Peace is laid before him. He lifts it up, partly un-sheathes it, and asks, in Welsh, three times: 'Is it peace?'

Each time he receives the answer 'Heddwch!' (Peace!) from the assembled crowds.

The highlights of the festival are the Crowning of the Bard, when the composer of the winning poem receives the Bardic Crown, and the Chairing of the Bard. Receiving the Bardic Crown is the greatest honour that a Welsh Bard can win, and the judges' standard is so high that there have been occasions when the prize has not been awarded. In 1953 a woman was the winner, for the first time in history.

Second Sunday in August   Souden,
Battle of Otterburn Commemoration   Roxburghshire, Scotland

In 1388 Scottish army leaders met at Souden Kirk to plan a raid on the English, in retaliation for an invasion that had taken place three years earlier. The resulting battle was fought at Otterburn in Northumberland. Hotspur, Earl of Northumberland, was defeated by the Earl of Douglas, who himself was killed on the night before the Scots were victorious. After the battle it is likely that the Scottish dead were buried in the churchyard at Souden, as it is the nearest consecrated ground from Otterburn over the Scottish border.

The church of Souden is now in ruins, but an annual open-air service is held there to commemorate the valour of the Scots. During this service the flag of 'Red Douglas'—a red heart on yellow cloth—is draped over the fallen stones.

Monday after August 12th (Feast of St. Marwenne)
Marhamchurch Revel   Marhamchurch, near Bude, Cornwall

The Celtic saint Marwenne is reputed to have brought Christianity to this Cornish village in the sixth century, and the annual Revel is held on the Monday after her Feast Day. Father Time crowns the Queen of the Revel outside the church where the saint is supposed to have had her cell. The Queen on horseback, led by a brass band and followed by her attendants, processes to the Revel ground, where there are sideshows, competitions and Cornish wrestling.

Third week in August   Innerleithen,
Cleiking the Devil   Peeblesshire, Scotland

The Cleikum ceremonies of Innerleithen have evolved from the St. Ronan Border Games, which were founded about 150 years ago by Sir Walter Scott, John Lockhart and James Hogg, the poet. They perpetuate the legend of the seventh-century monk St. Ronan, who overcame the Devil by his teaching. This connection with education is upheld by the choice of the Dux, or head boy, of the local school to play St. Ronan. He carries the Cleikum Crozier and is charged with keeping St. Ronan's banner unsullied. His attendant 'monks' carry staffs; the youngest, a 'lay brother', guides the procession with a lantern.

First the Runic Cross is visited and two schoolboy 'monks' address their 'saint'. St. Ronan washes his hands with water from the Spa well and then 'cleiks the Devil'—that is, he catches hold of the Devil's hind leg with his crozier as a reminder of St. Ronan's struggle with his adversary 1,200 years ago. 'St. Ronan' then releases a flock of pigeons, and the day ends with a torchlight procession.

On the last day of the festivities there are traditional games. The Saint and his attendant monks climb Caerlea Hill for the rite of burning an effigy of the Devil on a pyre. Hundreds of torches are lit from the burning pyre and the procession returns to Innerleithen to the music of bagpipes. Once again St. Ronan has vanquished the forces of evil.

August 24th   Gulval,
Blessing of the Mead   St. Mount's Bay, Cornwall

August 24th is St. Bartholomew's Day, and he is the patron saint of bee-keepers and honey-makers. It was customary for the honey crop to be taken on St. Bartholomew's Day, and the day has therefore been chosen for the ceremony of Blessing the Mead (of which honey is the principal ingredient) to honour the successful revival of the ancient industry of mead-making.

It is conducted by the Almoner of the Worshipful Company of Mead Makers, who is the vicar of the parish. The ceremony starts with a church service, after which the participants transfer to the Mead Hall, which is the Company's Livery Hall. The Almoner blesses the mead (which has been fermenting for two years) and pours it into the St. Ives Loving Cup. It is then transferred to a vat.

The drinking of mead has always been something of a ceremonial occasion. In Roman times it was offered to the gods of love and fertility. Few people today believe that drinking mead will help a marriage to be happy and fruitful, but it is still supposed to have curative medicinal qualities.

In England mead used to be drunk from a 'mazer', a bowl made from pickled birds-eye maple wood. The rim was mounted with silver and the finished object was a very beautiful example of skilled craftsmanship.

Last Sunday in August   Eyam,
Plague Sunday   Derbyshire

When the plague of 1665–66 was at its height in London a parcel of clothing was sent from the stricken capital to a tailor in the small village of Eyam. On Wakes Sunday members of the tailor's family began to fall ill. They soon died, other villagers followed them, and the death roll mounted rapidly. The Rector of Eyam, William Mompesson, persuaded his parishioners to embark on a heroic line of action. This was for Eyam to become a voluntary prison from which nobody would try to escape, in order that the plague should not spread beyond the confines of the village. It was a remarkable example of communal heroism, for those who had not succumbed to the disease could easily have left home, but they knew that by doing so they might well carry the seeds of sickness with them. The Duke of Devonshire, who owned Eyam, arranged for food to be left at the village boundary, and the able men and women carried it to their suffering neighbours.

For months the plague persisted. It died down for a while but returned in the spring of 1666 and lasted until the autumn of that year, and during that time the people of Eyam bravely suffered its ravages, their only consolation being the knowledge that their isolation was preventing it from spreading. The church was closed; the rector preached from a rock in a hollow called Cucklet Delf. Three-quarters of the population of 350 or so died, but no case of infection was reported from anywhere outside the parish.

An open-air service is now held in Eyam every Wakes Sunday in Cucklet Delf in memory of William Mompesson and his self-sacrificing parishioners. A band leads a procession of Anglican and Nonconformist clergy and their congregations from the church to the clearing in the wood. A special *Plague Hymn* is sung and an address given.

September to December

Harvest

Thanksgiving for the harvest is one of the oldest and most joyous festivals that man has created. It is the fulfilment of his urgent need to provide the means of life for himself and his family—the relief of seeing the fruition of the crops he has so lovingly and fearfully planted under the supervision of auspicious gods. Most of the pagan customs that gathered round the harvest season have either disappeared or have sunk under the weight of Christian disapproval and have radically changed. Today, the climax of the season is the picturesque but genteel Harvest Festival celebrated in churches. Ladies sing 'We plough the fields and scatter the good seed on the land', and farmers proclaim that all is safely gathered in, often after the worst harvest in living memory.

A Harvest Festival gives its participants a cosy feeling of security and permanence, that it has all been going on for centuries and always will, but in fact the present form of celebration is little more than a hundred years old. It is a Victorian innovation, started by the Rev. R. S. Hawker, vicar of Morwenstow in Cornwall, who, in 1843, invited his parishioners to receive the Sacrament in 'the bread of the new corn'.

However innocuous harvest rites are today, they are a relic of the great drama of the season when the fruits of the earth were collected and the means of life ensured for another year, and the thankfulness had a hidden stratum of cruelty.

The leading role in the drama was taken by Ceres, the Roman corn-goddess. In Britain she was later known by several names: the Maiden, the Harvest Queen, the Kern or Corn Baby, the Kern Doll, the Ivy Girl, the Neck and the Mare. Sometimes she was simply the stalks of corn; sometimes she was represented by a sheaf dressed in many-coloured clothes which were decorated with flowing ribbons and the finest lace. Whatever her form, she dominated the banquets, harvest suppers and merry-making of early times.

The Kern Baby, or whatever name she was known by locally, was made either from the last of the corn left standing, which was ceremonially cut with great respect, or from the biggest and ripest ears to be found in the field. The task of cutting the final sheaf was not eagerly sought after, for the spirit herself dwelt in the corn, and mere mortals shirked the responsibility of cutting her down. So often the act was left to chance. All those present threw their sickles at the lone sheaf from a respectable distance, thus no one could be said to have deliberately performed the act. In the depths of folk memory there was still the awareness of the death and resurrection cycle. The vegetation deity of the remote past needed to be propitiated by a human sacrifice.

Once the deed was done the triumph of achievement was experienced. All *was* safely gathered in, and it was time to rejoice. The Kern Baby was made and held aloft, and was carried with great ceremony to the place where the supper was going to be held, usually in the farmer's biggest barn.

The harvest supper was the culmination of the farming year. It was the farmer's expression of thanks to all his workers for their efforts to bring the harvest to a successful conclusion. All distinctions between master and servant were forgotten for this evening as everybody settled down, under the guardianship of the Kern Baby, to eat and drink their fill of ham, roast beef, vegetables, fruit, puddings, and an unlimited supply of beer and cider. The farmer's wife and the prettiest girls of the village served the food. Afterwards there were songs, games and gifts for all, and a sense of good fellowship pervaded the proceedings.

When the feast was over the Kern Baby was taken to the farm-house and kept there until the next harvest supper. The symbol of the previous year's harvest was ceremoniously burned in the farmyard.

The Kern Baby is by no means extinct, and can be seen in some churches as part of the Harvest Festival decorations, though she has been divested of her divine powers. At Little Waltham in Essex and Whalton in Northumberland, for example, Kern Babies are attached to one of the pews, and at

Overbury in Worcestershire a decorated conical figure, representative of the former goddess, is hung in the church porch. In one form or another she can be found hanging from the gables of thatched farmhouses or fastened to hayricks in many parts of the country.

In the north of England the harvest supper used to be called Mell Supper—'mell' from 'meal'—and in Northumberland especially the festivities included a charade in which some of the farm workers dressed up and pretended to be gate-crashers at the party. They were called 'guisers', and their disguise led to a good deal of friendly horseplay.

In some places the cart which brought home the last load of corn, with the Kern Baby in pride of place, was called the

Hockey Cart. A girl in white rode the leading horse, and it was a sight that must have been familiar to Robert Herrick when he wrote:

> *Come forth, my Lord, and see the Cart,*
> *Drest up with all the country art.*
> *See here a Maukin, there a sheet*
> *As spotless pure as it is sweet;*
> *The horses, mares, and frisking fillies,*
> *(Clad, all, in linnen, white as lillies,)*
> *The harvest swaines and wenches bound*
> *For joy, to see the Hock-cart crown'd.*

Enthusiastic villagers, awaiting the appearance of the Hockey Cart, would douse the reapers with water, thus perpetuating an age-old rain-making device to ensure plentiful rain for the next year's crops. A seed cake, baked at harvest time and given to the harvesters, was called the Hockey Cake.

The custom of 'crying the neck', once prevalent in the west of England, is still observed here and there, though now it is incorporated in the Harvest Festival held in the church. The origin of the word 'neck' or 'nack' is obscure. It may come from an old Norse word for a sheaf of corn, or it may have a connection with 'nix', a water spirit that is supposed to be from where we get Old Nick, one of the Devil's names.

The Devon version of 'crying the neck' is described in Brand's *Popular Antiquities*. While the labourers were reaping the last field of wheat, one of them went to each group of sheaves and selected the best of the ears, which he then tied up neatly, 'plaiting and arranging the straws most tastefully'. When the labourers' work was done and the last of the wheat cut, the entire company of reapers, binders and gleaners would form a circle round the man with the neck. He then stooped down, grasped the neck with both hands, and held it near to the earth. The people surrounding him removed their hats and held them downwards, too, a gesture of homage to the soil which had nurtured the crops. Then everybody rose slowly and held their arms and hats above their heads. The man with the neck did the same. This action was accompanied by a prolonged cry of 'The neck! The neck! The neck!' Then, with the same arm and body movements, they cried out, 'Wee yen! Wee yen! Wee yen!' Then the company burst out into boisterous laughter, and hats were flung up into the air. One of the men seized the neck and ran with it as fast as he could to the farmhouse door, where one of the maids was waiting with a bucket of water near by.

'If,' says Brand, 'the holder of the neck could contrive to get into the house otherwise than by the door at which the girl stood, he could lawfully kiss her; if, however, he,failed, he was regularly soused with the contents of the bucket.' This, obviously, was another manifestation of ritual rain-making.

Brand explains the cries of 'Wee yen! Way yen!' as the local dialect for 'We end', meaning the end of harvest. A more modern interpretation is 'I have 'un' and 'What have ye?' It was every farmer's aim to be the first in the parish to finish cutting the corn, and an air of triumph is undoubtedly felt in the full-throated cries.

In the neighbourhood of Ilfracombe 'crying the neck' continued until the last years of the nineteenth century. There the neck was made of four plaits of wheat and was as thick as a man's wrist. It resembled a doll with a narrow waist and full skirt. Kingsbridge celebrated the harvest by 'crying the neck' up to 1930, and Martinhoe until 1949. A form of the custom was made part of the Harvest Festival celebrations at Breage, in Cornwall, in 1962.

In Hertfordshire the corn-goddess was called the Mare. Here, when she had retreated to her last refuge, the few remaining blades of corn were tied together and the reapers threw their sickles at them in order to kill the spirit at a distance. The man who succeeded called out 'I have her!' 'What have you?' cried the others. 'A Mare, a Mare, a Mare!' was the reply. The others asked him what he was going to do with it, and were told that he was going to send it to a neighbouring farmer who had not finished cutting his corn.

Most counties had their own special way of celebrating the 'in-gathering', but they all sprang from the same pre-Christian impulse, the act of sacrifice which had to be performed at the end of the harvest. As it was necessary to cut the corn and bury the seed, so the corn spirit had to be killed in order that she could rise again in the spring with the growing crops. The cries when the neck was held up were originally the wails of death, and the shouting and dancing which followed captured the joy of resurrection.

The Ivy Girl of Kent was a human-shaped figure made from the best of the corn. In Scotland it was called the Maiden and was cut by the youngest girl who was helping with the harvest. In the north-east of Scotland it was called the 'Cailleach' or Old Woman, and was dressed to look the part. The Cailleach occupied a place of honour at the feast. It was toasted by the company and swirled around the dance floor by the local lads.

In Yorkshire, church bells rang morning and evening during the harvest. In Hertfordshire there was horn-blowing. In parts of East Anglia an amusing custom called 'Hallooing largesse' was observed. The Lord of the Harvest, who had been appointed by his fellow labourers for his skill in reaping and binding, led the company round the village and they joined hands in a circle before various houses. Bowing their heads towards the centre of the ring they shouted, 'Holla, holla, holla!', then, rising to a crescendo, 'Largesse!' On receiving 'largesse' from the person they had serenaded, they passed on to the next house and repeated the cries.

Monday after Wakes Sunday
(the first Sunday after September 4th)   Abbots Bromley,
Abbots Bromley Horn Dance   near Rugely, Staffordshire

A unique dance, the only one of its kind in Europe, is performed at Abbots Bromley. The Horn Dance is a processional dance which lasts the whole day. It starts at dawn from outside the village church and it tours the countryside, visiting farms where the dancers are welcomed as bringers of good luck and fertility to the crops. After twenty strenuous miles it ends in the main street, and refreshment is taken at one of the inns.

There are six dancers, a Fool, a Hobby-horse, which is also known as Robin Hood, Maid Marian the Man-Woman, a Bowman who is a youth with an arrow and crossbow which he snaps in time to the music, and two musicians, one playing the melodeon, the other the triangle. The Hobby-horse, too, beats time by snapping its hinged jaws. The uniqueness of the dance lies in the horns that are mounted on stout poles and carried by the dancers so that they rest on their shoulders. The heads and antlers are carved wooden replicas of the reindeer, an animal long extinct in this country. Three sets are painted white, and three black. They are so heavy that the dancers cannot perform any elaborate steps, and the dance is a very dignified one.

The dancers are dressed in jerkins over green shirts, patterned breeches and wide berets. They set out on their route in single file. Every so often the leader doubles back, after having led the men into a circle, and cuts through the line so that the blacks and whites are face to face. Then the set dance is performed. During it the blacks and whites engage in symbolic combat, advancing towards each other with horns fiercely dipped, then retreating and advancing again until the lines ultimately cross and change over. The black leader then breaks away and starts the procession again. The rest follow in single file with the Bowman at the tail, snapping his arrow as though shooting at the escaping Animal-Men.

The Horn Dance contains elements of both Morris and sword dances, but differs from both of them. It is of great antiquity. The earliest account of it we have was given by Robert Plot in *The Natural History of Staffordshire*, published in 1686. One local explanation of its origin is that it celebrates the restoration of hunting rights to the common people in medieval times, but it is clearly very much older than that. It may be a relic of a hunting dance, although why reindeer horns are used is something of a mystery. It would have to be a very long folk memory to remember hunting an animal that has been extinct for so long in Britain. The presence of the Man-Woman suggests that a fertility rite was once part of it. 'She' carries two wooden implements symbolising the male and the female. The stylised battle of the Deer-Men perhaps represents the struggle between life and death.

But however mysterious its origins, the Horn Dance has survived in its present form because the Church adopted the pagan rites, adapted them and gave them its blessing. Not only does the first 'run' begin outside the church, but the horns are hung on the aisle wall and other properties are kept in the vestry when not in use, and money collected during the day's dancing is given towards the upkeep of the church. Replicas of the horns hang in Cecil Sharp House, the London head-quarters of the English Folk Dance and Song Society.

September 1st   Colchester,
Opening of the Oyster Fishing Season   Essex

The opening of the season (September is the first month with an 'R' in it since April) starts with an inspection of the Colne Oyster Fishery by the Mayor of Colchester, members of the Town Council and representatives of the Fishery Board, who all go out from Brightlingsea in a fishing smack. The Town Clerk reads out the ancient proclamation of 1256 which declares that the fishing rights of the River Colne belong to the Corporation of the Borough of Colchester. Then those present drink a toast to the Queen in gin, and gingerbread is eaten. The Mayor, in full regalia, lowers the first trawl in Pyefleet Creek to bring up the first oysters, and the season is then officially open.

Second Friday in September   Musselburgh,
Fishermen's Walk   Midlothian, Scotland

The Fishermen's Walk is the harvest festival of the fisher-folk, a thanksgiving held at the end of the fishing season. At Musselburgh, Cockenzie, Fisherrow and other places in Scotland the villages are decorated with garlands and flags for the Walk Day. The fishing fleet lies at its moorings and local bands provide music for dancing in the streets. The Walk starts shortly after midday. Women and girls wear striped petticoats, a turned-back overdress and a shawl. They carry small dolls which are also dressed as fisher-wives, and a large doll is carried at the head of the procession. The walkers finish up at the field where sports and games are to be held for the rest of the day.

Saturday nearest September 8th   Lichfield,
The Lichfield Sheriff's Ride   Staffordshire

Lichfield's charter, granted in 1553, stipulates that a Sheriff must be elected on July 25th, St. James's Day, every year. If the proposed man refuses office he is liable to a fine, imprisonment and loss of citizenship. On election he must make a tour of the city's boundaries on the Feast of the Nativity of the Blessed Virgin Mary in order to make sure that the boundary stones are still in place.

The annual Sheriff's Ride has taken place, with few breaks, since the charter was granted. Before the event the local newspapers carry an invitation to the citizens of Lichfield to accompany the Sheriff.

The Ride starts about 11 a.m., and those taking part go on horseback round the twenty-four miles of the boundaries, halting at the old boundary marks, or where they once stood, stopping occasionally for refreshment. Men posted at various places keep a lookout for anyone who might be tempted to cut short his journey.

After the Ride, the Sheriff is escorted back to the Guildhall by the City Sword and Mace-bearers.

Saturday nearest September 18th   Lichfield,
Doctor Johnson Commemoration   Staffordshire

Samuel Johnson was born at Lichfield on September 18th, 1709, and the town remembers its famous son with suitable pageantry. First the Johnson statue in the market square is visited by a civic procession which includes the Mayor, Sheriffs, Recorder, Mace-bearers, Sword-bearer, clergy from the cathedral, members of the Johnson Society and visitors from overseas. A laurel wreath is laid at the foot of the statue, and the choir sings hymns and recites the Johnson Prayer from the steps of the house where he was born.

In the evening a commemoration supper is held by candlelight. The main course is steak and kidney pudding with mushrooms, or saddle of mutton, followed by apple tart and cream, which was the Doctor's favourite meal. The guests drink ale and hot punch, served by Mace-bearers dressed in eighteenth-century costume. After supper they smoke church-warden pipes.

At Uttoxeter, eighteen miles from Lichfield, Doctor Johnson is remembered by the children of the town, because of a ceremony in the market-place which was initiated just over a hundred years ago by Nathaniel Hawthorne, the American novelist. During a visit to Uttoxeter he discovered to his surprise that the local children did not know the story of Doctor Johnson's penance in the market-place and decided to rectify the omission.

Michael Johnson, Samuel's father, had a bookstall in Uttoxeter market. Samuel's refusal to help him to run the stall was the cause of a serious quarrel between them, which had not been healed when the father died. As a penance for his unfilial behaviour Samuel stood bareheaded in the rain for several hours on the spot in the market-place where his father's stall had stood.

Children are told the story on the anniversary of Doctor Johnson's birth, and one of them is chosen to hang a wreath over the memorial plaque which marks the site of Michael Johnson's bookstall.

September 19th   Richmond,
First Fruits of the Harvest   Yorkshire

At Richmond the Mayor is Clerk of the Market, and as such has absolute jurisdiction over both open and covered markets. On Saturday, which is market day, two halberds are placed outside his office to show that he is available if wanted. Every year, on September 19th, the Mayor presents two bottles of wine to the first farmer of the district who takes a sample of the new season's wheat to the Market Cross. A corn expert is present to make sure that the corn is indeed wheat and is a fair sample of the harvest. Before the wine is presented there is a thanksgiving service in Holy Trinity Church, which stands in the centre of the cobbled market-place.

The farmer opens one bottle so that the Mayor's health can be drunk. He takes the other bottle home for a private celebration.

Richmond has other old customs which are faithfully observed. The Prentice Bell is rung every morning at 8 a.m. and the Curfew is sounded at 8 p.m. Another bell, the Pancake Bell, is heard once a year. It is rung at 10.55 a.m. on Shrove Tuesday to remind housewives that it is time to start making their pancake mixture in readiness for the midday meal.

When an inhabitant of Richmond dies, the bell of Holy Trinity Tower is tolled—nine times for a man, six for a woman and three for a child. A card bearing the name of a deceased child and the date of death is posted on the door of the Town Hall.

Sunday nearest September 19th   Painswick,
Clipping the Church   Gloucestershire

There are more than a hundred yew trees in the churchyard at Painswick, looking like giant green puffballs. On the Sunday nearest to September 19th, which is known as 'Clipping Sunday', a very old ceremony takes place. A procession of choir, children and adults, led by the town band, makes its way round the boundary of the churchyard, then the children form a a circle round the church itself and dance round it, moving towards the walls and back again several times as they sing the *Clipping Hymn*. A sermon is preached from the foot of the church tower, and the church is 'clipped' for another year. 'Clipping' means embracing, and has nothing to do with the trimming of the yew trees, though this takes place a few days before the ceremony, and the two events are often confused. There is a similar ceremony at Wirksworth in Derbyshire on the Sunday following September 8th.

September 25th   Ashton-under-Lyne,
Pageant of the Black Knight   Lancashire

According to tradition, Sir Ralph Assheton, Lord of the Manor of Middleton in the time of Henry VI, was the local tyrant. He rode round his parish once a year, fining or punishing his tenants if they had neglected their lands and allowed weeds to grow. The severity of his judgements made him feared and hated.

His son, a milder-mannered person, abolished the custom,

and when he died he left money to pay for an annual procession on Easter Monday to commemorate his father's misdeeds. The central figure was a Black Knight—an effigy in armour, set on horseback. The ceremony ended with the figure being shot at and pelted with missiles.

Nowadays the figure, after being paraded round the town accompanied by various medieval characters, is taken to Stamford Park and is there strung up on the Old Cross.

Michaelmas

Michaelmas Day, September 29th, is the Feast of St. Michael and all Angels. In spite of the formidable character of St. Michael, however, most of the folk customs associated with his day are no longer practised. Michaelmas tends rather to bring to mind the type of aster known as Michaelmas Daisy, or here and there the traditional feast of Michaelmas goose.

September 29th is also a Quarter Day, when certain rents and accounts are due for payment, and it is the day on which the Lord Mayor of London is elected.

On St. Michael's Eve a few customs reminiscent of Hallowmas used to be observed—nut-cracking in Surrey, bonfires in Lincolnshire, church porch-watching in Yorkshire. But these were not widespread and the reason for their displacement from the usual season is obscure.

Until 1845 a curious Michaelmas custom took place at Kidderminster in Worcestershire. Crowds assembled in the main streets about 3 p.m. and, on a signal from the Town Hall bell, began to observe a 'lawless hour' by throwing cabbage stalks at each other. For the next hour law and order was suspended, and whatever damage was done could not result in the arrest of the person responsible for it. It is hard to believe that on such a high-spirited occasion the objects that were thrown would be confined to cabbage stalks; other rubbish from the vegetable market would no doubt be added to the ammunition.

This was the day when the new Bailiff of the town was elected, and if one equates the Bailiff and the Corporation, as guardians of civil rights, with the guardian angels to whom the day is dedicated, the lawless hour might well have commemorated the change of power from the retiring Bailiff to the newly elected one, a period when, so to speak, no one was in charge. At 4 p.m., when the lawless hour was over, the Bailiff-elect and the Corporation, preceded by drums and fifes, appeared, in order to visit the retiring Bailiff. This procession was pelted, too, not with cabbage stalks but with apples, and not by the mob, but by the most respectable families of the neighbourhood. 'I have known,' says a writer in *The Gentleman's Magazine* in 1790, 'forty pots of apples expended at one house.'

Another violent custom took place at Bishop's Stortford in Hertfordshire on Old Michaelmas Day (October 10th). It was called Ganging Day. In the morning a number of young men gathered in the fields to choose their leader. Then they followed him wherever he led them, through ponds, hedges and ditches. Whenever they met anyone, man or woman, two of the gang would grab the unfortunate person by the arms and 'bump' him—that is, swing him against any handy object, such as tree, gatepost or house side. If two people were encountered they were bumped against each other. Sensible and respectable women usually made a point of staying at home on Ganging Day.

October 20th   Colchester,
Oyster Festival   Essex

Richard I granted the valuable Colne Oyster Fishing privilege to the citizens of Colchester, and a feast to commemorate the event has been held annually for hundreds of years.

Until 1752 the feast took place on October 8th, the eve of St. Denys's Day, but the date was changed to October 20th when the calendar was rearranged. After the proclamation of the fair in each of the four wards of the town, the Mayor, Aldermen and members of the Council return in procession to the Town Hall where the feast is held. Between three hundred and four hundred guests are invited. Royalty has often attended.

A Year of Festivals

October 23rd (or near)   Redcliffe,
The Redcliffe Pipe Walk   Bristol

In 1190 Robert de Berkeley made a gift of spring water to
the church of St. Mary Redcliffe. The water now runs in a pipe,
the course of which is marked by fourteen stones. It goes
through Redcliffe and Barminster up to Knowle, where the
spring rises. Every year the vicar and parishioners of St.
Mary Redcliffe assert their right to the water by walking over
its underground course, as far as they can.

At each stone a member of the walk is 'bumped'. The walk
ends at St. Barnabas's Church, which is near the source of the
spring, and the walkers take tea in the church hall. At one point
the pipe passes under a railway line and until about thirty-five
years ago trains were stopped so that the line could be crossed
in safety. Nowadays the walkers have to make a detour.

Hallowmas

The three days between October 31st and November 2nd see
pagan and Christian celebrations intertwined in a fascinating
way. All Hallow's Eve, usually called Hallowe'en, is followed
by All Hallow's Day, which is also All Saints' Day. The next
day is All Souls' Day, and the three-day period is a perfect
example of superstition struggling with religious belief. The
pre-Christian aspect is concerned with the festival of Samhain,
which celebrated the end of summer and the beginning of the
Celtic New Year on November 1st. This was a time of darkness
and mystery, when ghosts and witches were abroad and winter
was near.

At Hallowmas the Beltane fires of spring were lit again from
the 'need-fire'; that is, they were rekindled by means of friction,
such as that between tinder and flint, to drive away evil influ-
ences and to give symbolic energy to the dying sun. Household
fires were started from the new flames.

Hallowmas, too, was a time for divination and prying into
the unknown, for avoiding witches at their sabbaths, for ritual
games, and, as the bells pealed out, for remembering the dead
and all those saints who had no special day of their own.

The fires of Hallowe'en burned strongest in Scotland and

Ireland, where the Celtic influence was most pronounced, although they lingered on in some of the northern counties of England until the early years of this century. In England the day of fires became November 5th, the anniversary of the Gunpowder Plot of 1605, but its proximity to Hallowe'en is more than coincidence. Beltane and Bonfire Night have a common origin.

The Hallowe'en fires brought comfort to souls in purgatory and people prayed for them as they held burning straw up high. They protected their homes against witches by having large fires in the grates, and round the hearth families thrilled to tales of ghosts. Children played their special Hallowe'en games, and girls went to fantastic means to find out who they were going to marry.

Duck-apple and Snap-apple were, and still are, the two most popular games of the season. In the former, apples are placed in a bowl of water and the contestants, sometimes blindfolded, must take a bite from one of the apples without using their hands. It is not permitted to edge the apple to the side of the bowl to get a purchase on it. There is a nice complication in one version of the game in which the player holds a fork between his teeth and tries to spear the apple with it.

The same 'no hands' rule also applies to Snap-apple, and it

is equally difficult to take a bite when the fruit is suspended on a long piece of string. The over-eager is likely to receive a sharp bang on the face from the swinging apple. A variation of the game is to fix an apple and a lighted candle at opposite ends of a stick suspended horizontally and to swing the stick round. The object is to catch the elusive apple between the teeth without getting either singed or spattered with grease—or finding that one has a mouthful of candle instead of fruit. It is of little importance to the children who enjoy these games that they are participating in an ancient custom of honouring the fruit at the end of apple-gathering.

Apples, nuts and candles figure prominently in many of the divinations that were practised at Hallowe'en. A girl who threw an apple pip named after her sweetheart on to the fire would know, according to how it burned, whether he loved her or not. If a girl had more than one suitor, the rivalry between them was transferred to two pips, one stuck on each of the girl's cheeks; the last to fall off indicated which of the young men loved her truly. An apple placed under the pillow would bring a girl dreams of her sweetheart.

Brand cites a rather more elaborate method of divination which was used in Scotland. 'Take a candle and go along to a looking-glass; eat an apple before it, and some traditions say, you should comb your hair all the time; the face of your conjugal companion to be, will be seen in the glass, as if peeping over your shoulder.' If a thrifty maiden wanted to use the whole apple, having stuck the pips on her cheeks and eaten the flesh before her looking-glass, she could then throw the peel over her left shoulder with her right hand, and it would fall to form the initial of her future husband's name.

In parts of the north of England Hallowe'en was known as Nut-crack Night. Nuts were put on the fire and, according to their behaviour in the flames, forecast faithfulness (or the opposite) in sweethearts, marriage dates, and the success or failure of the marriage. Eggs were also used. The end of an egg was pricked and the drops of albumen were allowed to fall into water. The resulting shapes conveyed information about future marriage partners. In Cornwall molten lead was dropped into cold water, and this divulged the trade that the husband-to-be-followed. An inquisitive watcher at a church porch would see the face of her future marriage partner or, what must have been very unwelcome, the faces of those people who were to die during the coming year.

Places as far apart as Exmoor in Somerset and Sutherland and Caithness in Scotland combined Hallowe'en with Mischief Night, when boys played all kinds of practical jokes on their neighbours. They changed shop signs, took gates off their hinges, whitewashed doors, and tied door latches; and the maliciously-minded used the opportunity to take revenge on those with whom they had quarrelled.

Frightening witches away was a widespread custom. The method employed is still in use, though its purpose is different. A turnip or mangel-wurzel was hollowed out, eye and mouth holes were cut through the skin and a lighted candle placed inside. This horrid creation was left in a strategic position, fixed to a gatepost or a tree, and witches and evil spirits were supposed to take the hint and steer clear. Nowadays turnip lanterns are intended to scare human, rather than supernatural, beings.

Last Thursday in October   Hinton St. George,
Punkie Night   Somerset

On Punkie Night (a punkie is a lantern) the children of the village form into groups and walk through the streets singing their *Punkie Night Song*, knocking on doors and asking for money or candles to put into their hollowed-out mangel-wurzels. The lanterns are often carved with beautiful and elaborate designs. Sometimes they are cut to resemble faces and stuck on a pole draped with a white cloth.

Souling
   'A Soule-cake, a Soule-cake, have mercy on all Christian Soules for a Soule-cake'

In the Christian calendar All Saints' Day is dedicated to those saints without special days of dedication of their own. At one time church bells rang out on All Saints' Eve, and it was believed that this would give aid to all the souls in purgatory. Henry VIII put a stop to such 'superstitious practices', and in the 1630s the churchwardens at York were asked 'whether there be any within your parish or chapelry that used to ring bells superstitiously upon any abrogated holiday, or the eves thereof?'

When the fear that the sound of bells would lead an innocent hearer straight into the arms of Rome had passed, the custom was revived by many parish priests. In course of time the Feast of All Souls was accepted by the Anglican Church.

The custom of souling, that is, begging for specially made cakes for the souls of the dead, was widely practised. Originally soul cakes were sent to friends and relatives of a deceased person. In some parts soulers begged for 'dole bread', but usually it was cake, a flat, round biscuit-like cake that was made from a light spiced mixture. Like so many old customs that survived, the pattern gradually changed. The actual cakes became rarer, and soulers were given sweets or money. The original motive for giving was forgotten, and all that now remains is the skeleton of a custom, lacking in meaning or importance.

Children are now the only soulers, although until the early years of the century grown men and old women were just as likely to take the opportunity of adding to their financial or liquid assets. In 1880 the *Cheshire Sheaf* reported that 'three middle-aged men, with a concertina, have just been souling here. They began well but ended with very bad verses about ale and strong beer which, they said, was all for which they came'.

Children who go souling sing songs which follow a similar pattern. They can be seen and heard in Cheshire, north Shropshire, and along the Staffordshire border. This example comes from Market Drayton:

> *Soul, soul, for a soul cake!*
> *I pray, good missis, for a soul cake!*
> *An apple or pear, a plum or a cherry,*
> *Any good thing to make us merry.*

(*left*) Rush-
bearing in
Lancashire

Plate 9

(*below*) Cheese-
rolling at
Cooper's Hill,
Gloucestershire

(*upper*) Abbots Bromley Horn Dance, Staffordshire. Head and antlers of reindeer
(*lower*) Abbots Bromley Horn Dance in progress

Plate 10

(left) A harvest cart

Plate 11

(below) The Paper Boys, Marshfield, Gloucestershire

(above) The Mayor officiating at the opening of the Colchester Oyster Season

Plate 12

(right) The Town Sergeant at the opening of the Colchester Oyster Season

One for Peter, two for Paul,
Three for Him who made us all.
Up with the kettle and down with the pan,
Give us good alms and we'll be gone!

In other soul songs there are requests for ale, strong beer, or silver money, and they usually contain verses thanking the donor and wishing health and long life to him, his family, workmen and livestock.

In Cheshire, souling was enlivened by the presence of the Hodening Horse—a man dressed in a white sheet and a horse's head with hinged jaws that snapped fiercely. 'Hoden' rhymes with 'wooden', and its origin is obscure. It may be derived from the Norse god Odin, but it is more likely to be associated with Robin Hood when he became one of the characters in the May Games. How the horse sacrifice of the Norsemen became part of a Christian rite remembering the souls of the dead is a mystery.

A form of mummers' play, called the Soul Caking Play, is still performed in Cheshire on All Souls' Day. Until the First World War it could be seen in several villages, but it is now confined to Comberbach and Antrobus. It is the only version of a mumming play which includes a horse. At Comberbach, north of Northwich, the Hodening Horse is called the Wild Horse. It is supposed to be a descendant of Marbury Dun, a famous racehorse which is buried in the grounds of Marbury Hall. It is built on an actual horse's skull, and has movable jaws. The play contains the traditional characters, but they are unusual in that they wear modern clothes. King George fights the Black Prince, and the Quack Doctor heals the latter's wounds. Beelzebub, a comic figure with club and dripping-pan, tells his tall stories, and the Wild Horse is praised for its equine virtues.

Bonfire Night
> *Remember, remember, the fifth of November,*
> *Gunpowder, treason and plot.*
> *I see no reason why gunpowder treason*
> *Should ever be forgot.*

Not that anyone in England is likely to forget the fifth of November! For weeks beforehand, Roman candles, squibs, rockets and penny demons have been hoarded. Old clothes have been collected for the guy. Orange boxes, gates and old chairs have been stored, ready for the bonfire. Children everywhere have been exhibiting their rag-stuffed effigies and begging for 'a penny for the guy'. Bonfire Night is celebrated as fervently and noisily as ever, even though the motive is not, as it once was, rejoicing at the frustration of a Popish plot.

Some of its former vigour has disappeared, fortunately. 'In my youthful days,' says a writer in *The Every-Day Book*, 'when Guy met Guy—then came a tug of war! The partisans fought, and a decided victory ended in the capture of the Guy belonging to the vanquished. Sometimes desperate bands, who omitted, or were without the means to make Guys, went forth like Froissart's knights upon adventures. An enterprise of this sort was called "going to *smug* a Guy", that is, to steal one by force of arms, fists and sticks, from its rightful owners. These partisans were always successful, for they always attacked the weak.'

The fun and games that the butchers of Clare Market enjoyed has disappeared, too, and they no longer thrash at each other round about the wood fire 'with the strongest sinews of slaughtered bulls'; nor do they parade the streets 'ringing peals from marrow-bones and cleavers, so loud as to overpower the storms of sound that came from the rocking belfries of the churches. Many were the overthrow of carriages, from the discharge of hand-rockets, and the pressure of moving mobs inflamed to violence by drink, and fighting their way against each other.'

The conspiracy that is commemorated on November 5th was set in motion by a group of fanatical Roman Catholics led by Robert Catesby, Robert Winter and John Wright. Their aim was to blow up the Houses of Parliament on the day the king was to open Parliament. They were later joined by Guy Fawkes and others. They took a house adjoining the House of Lords, and in December 1604 began tunnelling from the cellar towards the Lords. After nearly a year they reached a vault and stored there thirty-six barrels of gunpowder.

Ten days before the explosion was due, however, Lord Monteagle, a Roman Catholic peer, received an anonymous letter, which at first he thought was the work of a lunatic. A perfunctory search of the cellars beneath the House of Lords was made, but nothing suspicious was found. Another search was made at midnight of the day preceding the ceremonial opening of Parliament, and this time Guy Fawkes was discovered at his post, equipped with lantern, tinder box and matches. He openly admitted his intention of igniting the gunpowder, adding that he was sorry not to have succeeded. He was tortured and forced to reveal the names of his fellow plotters, all of whom were subsequently caught and executed.

Thus Protestant England was saved from the designs of the Papists, though, as a precaution, Parliament has been searched before every annual opening of Parliament ever since.

Up to the beginning of this century November 5th was often known as Pope Day, but there is little anti-popery about the festival these days. The bonfire is more important than the guy that sits on top. (At Guy Fawkes's old school in York it is considered bad form to burn the effigy of an old boy.)

Many local authorities organise official celebrations; those at Bridgwater in Somerset and Lewes in Sussex are spectacular.

November 5th   Lewes,
Bonfire Night Celebrations   Sussex

The impressive ceremony at Lewes has been famous for many years. The Bonfire Societies in the town are responsible for the arrangements. An effigy of Pope Paul IV joins that of Guy Fawkes. There are torchlight processions, bands, 'Bonfire Boys' in fancy dress, and songs and prayers round the fires. Lewes is one of the few places where the militant Protestant nature of the occasion is strong, and an eighteenth-century 'No Popery' banner is carried in the procession.

November 5th   Bridgwater,
Bonfire Night Celebrations   Somerset

The celebrations at Bridgwater are supposed to date back to the spontaneous demonstrations of loyalty made by the people of the town when they heard of the capture of the plotters in 1605. The festivities are enlivened by the setting-off of the famous Bridgwater squibs. At one time they were home-made, but are now commercially made to a special formula. The Carnival is financed by a series of entertainments given for several days before the great occasion.

A small but significant reminder that the fires of November 5th are very much older than Guy Fawkes is the making of a special kind of cake for Bonfire Night. In Yorkshire it is called parkin; in Lancashire and Derbyshire it was called harcake or tharcake. The ingredients are mainly oatmeal, butter and treacle, and as parkin it can still be bought. Har was one of the names of Odin, and the word appears in such Lancashire place-names as Hargrave and Hargate. In the making of harcake the memory of an old Norse festival was preserved. Tharcake suggests a feast in honour of Thor, held on November 5th. In Bradwell, Derbyshire, the Primitive Methodists used to hold a Tharcake Supper on the Saturday nearest to November 5th.

November 5th   Shebbear,
Turning the Devil's Boulder   North Devon

Beneath an old tree in the village square of Shebbear lies a huge stone, reddish in colour and a flattened oval in shape. In the evening of November 5th the village bellringers ring the church's six bells as a warning to evil spirits to keep away. Then, led by the vicar, they go to the square where men with ropes and crowbars are waiting to turn the great stone over. The ceremony is performed by the light of lanterns and torches, and when the stone has been heaved over the village will prosper for another year. If the stone remains in the same position for two years running, superstition says that bad luck will follow.

This custom has been observed for hundreds of years, and has no connection with Guy Fawkes. Legend has it that the Devil dropped the stone while on his way from Heaven to Hell, but in fact it is likely that it was either once connected with some long-forgotten pagan ritual or marks a holy spot near the entrance to the churchyard.

November 11th (St. Martin's Day)   Knightlow Hill,
Wroth Silver   Warwickshire

Knightlow Hill is a tumulus surrounded by four fir trees that, by tradition, are the memorials to four knights who were killed in battle and buried on the spot. It is also the old meeting-place of the Hundred of Knightlow. Before dawn every St. Martin's Day representatives of the twenty-five parishes that make up the Hundred meet the agent of the Duke of Buccleuch, the Lord of the Manor, and, after hearing the charter of assembly read to them, put sums of money (called Wroth Silver), varying from 1p to 10p, into the hollow top of a stone called Knightlow Cross.

Anyone who fails to pay his due is fined a pound for each penny not paid or presents a white bull with a red nose and red ears to the Duke. The ceremony is followed by breakfast at the *Old Dun Cow Inn* at Dunchurch.

November 11th   Fenny Stratford,
Firing the Poppers   Buckinghamshire

Poppers are pots made from gunmetal, each about seven inches high and weighing about twenty pounds. They are usually kept in the belfry of St. Martin's Church, which was founded in 1730 by Dr. Browne Willis, an antiquarian and Lord of the Manor. Every St. Martin's Day these six old guns are taken to a field, charged with gunpowder and fired by application of a long red-hot rod to the touch-holes. The first goes off at 8 a.m. and the others at four-hourly intervals.

The custom started after the death of Dr. Willis in 1760 to add excitement to the annual parish feast that he arranged in his will. Fenny Poppers are also fired to mark some special occasion of national rejoicing.

November 23rd   Laxton,
Court Leet   Nottinghamshire

Laxton, a small farming village, is one of the few places in the country which still has a Court Leet. Much of the farming land is made up of three large open fields, which are divided into strips from one to ten acres in size and which are shared between about twenty-five farmers. The ancient rotation of crops system of farming is still maintained: that is, one year corn, one year root-crops and the third year fallow.

On November 23rd, the foreman of the jury and the twelve jurors of the Court Leet tour the three fields to see that none of the ancient laws have been broken. They take stakes and tape measures with them to check boundaries. They inspect the crops and look for examples of bad farming. The court is held at the *Dovecote Inn* and there offenders are fined. Lunch is served, and the money from fines is spent on beer.

The Court Leet also settles the agricultural policy for the next year.

November 26th   Ashburton,
Ale Tasting   Devon

The office of Portreeve, the forerunner of Mayor, is over a thousand years old in Ashburton. The holder of the office is appointed in November at a Court Leet held in the oldest schoolroom in the country which is still in use, that of the chapel of St. Lawrence, founded in 1314. Also appointed are the Ale Tasters, Bread Weighers, Pig Drivers, Scavengers, and the Surveyors of Markets and Water Courses. These offices are more picturesque than important, but the Ale Tasters, who are accompanied by members of the Court Leet, have the privilege of visiting the town's inns and sampling the ale. If it is found to be satisfactory, the Portreeve presents the landlord with a sprig of evergreen to be hung over the door of the inn.

November 30th (St. Andrew's Day)   Eton College,
Wall Game   Buckinghamshire

The Eton Wall Game is a variety of Rugby football that has its own rules and is different from all others. It is played between Collegers and Oppidans. The former are scholarship boys who live in the old College; the latter live in boarding-houses in various parts of the town. ('Oppidans' means townspeople.)

The rules of the game are so mysterious that they puzzle even Etonians, though the players themselves presumably know what they are doing. The aim of the game is to 'boss' (score) a goal by getting the ball into the other side's 'calx'. At one end of the field this is a chalk mark on a garden wall; at the other end it is a mark on a tree. The play consists chiefly of scrimmages against a brick wall and a goal is rarely scored.

December 6th (St. Nicholas's Day)   Berden,
Enthroning the Boy Bishop   Essex

The custom of enthroning a Boy Bishop, who holds office from St. Nicholas's Day to December 28th (Holy Innocents' Day), goes back about a thousand years, and was once widespread both in England and on the Continent. It seems to have been a link with the Roman Saturnalia when servants changed place with their masters. The custom was suppressed by Henry VIII, revived by Mary, and abolished again by Elizabeth I. Today's ceremonies are revivals.

Formerly the Boy Bishop wore episcopal vestments, carried a crozier and took part in all services which did not require an ordained priest. He was assisted by other children. On his last day of office he preached a sermon and blessed his congregation. If a Boy Bishop died during this period he was buried with as much ceremony as if he had been a real bishop. There is an effigy of a Boy Bishop in full vestments in Salisbury Cathedral.

Today the Boy Bishop, who is often a choirboy, is allowed to wear the cope, mitre and other insignia of a bishop, but he does not take services.

Other places which elect a Boy Bishop include Edwinstowe in Nottinghamshire, Par in Cornwall, Bristol, and Pokesdown near Bournemouth.

December 18th   Londonderry,
Closing the Gates Ceremony   Northern Ireland

In 1688 James II invaded Ulster and personally led an army of 20,000 men to the walls of Protestant Londonderry, thus beginning a siege of the city that lasted 105 days.

Colonel Lundy, the governor of the city, wanted to surrender, and became so unpopular with the defenders that, according to tradition, he was lowered from the walls and allowed to join the Jacobites, whose cause he favoured.

His attempts to hand over the city were thwarted by thirteen apprentice boys who, against orders, closed the Ferryquay Gate in the face of the English army, and the inhabitants of Derry replied 'No surrender' to all suggestions by the commander of the besieging army that they should give in. The city was relieved after the people had undergone many hardships and thousands had died of starvation or disease. A ship called the *Mountjoy* broke the blockade of the River Foyle and managed to get food to the besieged people.

The celebrations of December 18th are in honour of the thirteen apprentices. They are organised by the Association of the Apprentice Boys of Derry in the form of an historical pageant, the highlight of which is the burning of an effigy of Colonel Lundy.

December 21st (St. Thomas's Day)   Old Bolingbroke,
Candle Auction   Lincolnshire

This curious auction is held in connection with a church land charity, which stipulated that a piece of land, called Poor Folks' Close, should be let every five years by candle auction. Nowadays it is held annually.

A tallow candle and a pin are two necessary ingredients of the ceremony. The auctioneer, who is either the vicar or the Chairman of the Parish Council, sticks a pin into the candle about an inch from the top. He then lights the candle, and the bidding begins. When the flame reaches the pin it drops out and no further bids are accepted. The last bidder before the pin falls becomes the tenant of the land for a year. The money produced is distributed to widows and the poor of the parish.

Similar candle auctions are held at Tatworth and Congresbury in Somerset, Grimston and Diseworth in Leicestershire, and at Aldermaston in Berkshire, where an acre of church land is let every third year.

December 24th   Dewsbury,
Tolling the Devil's Knell   Yorkshire

This unusual bell-ringing custom has been observed since the middle of the thirteenth century. If it were not carried out, legend says that the Devil would be free to do his 'best' in the parish for the next twelve months.

The bell used is known as Black Tom of Soothill. On Christmas Eve it is tolled four times in four sets of four, and then rung once for every year since the birth of Jesus.

December 26th   Marshfield,
Paper Boys   Gloucestershire

The mummers' play was revived at Marshfield in 1929, and is now performed five times every Boxing Day. The first performance is at 11 a.m. The performers differ from most mummers in that their costumes are decorated with paper streamers, and the play contains singing and dancing as well as mumming. The hero is King William, and he is supported by Little Man John, Saucy Jack and Tenpenny Nit. There is a procession round the streets led by the village crier ringing his bell.

Also on Boxing Day the Grenoside and Handsworth sword dance teams from Sheffield come out.

December 27th (St. John's Day)   Melrose,
Freemasons' Walk   Roxburghshire, Scotland

The walk of the Melrose Masons has been carried on since 1707. The event begins in the evening of St. John's Day, when members of the Masonic Lodge of Melrose St. John in full regalia, and carrying torches, meet in the yard of the *George and Abbotsford Hotel* and walk in procession to the market-place. They are led by banner-bearers and a silver band. They circle the Town Cross three times and then go to Melrose Abbey, where they perform the same ceremony round the nave. They then form a semicircle round the chancel and sing *The Flower of the Forest*, *Scots Wha Hae* and *Auld Lang Syne*. After an address by the chaplain the procession returns to the Town Cross and the ceremony is officially over—though St. John's Day continues to be celebrated in the town's inns.

December 31st   Llangynwyd, Glamorganshire,
Mari Lwyd (Holy Mary) Mummers   South Wales

The mummers of Llangynwyd appear in fantastic dresses, the leader wearing a horse's skull decorated with ribbons. They call at selected houses and sing their traditional songs. The householder first refuses to allow them to enter, but eventually relents and provides the customary hospitality.

December 31st   Allendale,
Tar Burning   Northumberland

This ceremony, which has decidedly pagan origins, takes place on New Year's Eve. A procession of men in fancy dress—'guisers'—goes through the parish, each man carrying a wooden tub of burning tar on his head. At midnight a bonfire is lit and there is dancing round it. Then the men go off as first-footers to let in the New Year.

First-footing

First-footing, which is still popular in Scotland and the north of England, is performed in order to bring luck and prosperity to a household. The first person to enter a house on January 1st should be a dark stranger carrying a piece of coal, which he puts on the fire. He should be given bread or cake to eat and wine or whisky to drink; in this way the family is ensured of food and drink during the coming year.

Sometimes the stranger carries a sprig of mistletoe as well as coal, and he places bread and salt on the table, the traditional symbols of welcome and friendship. The whole ceremony should take place in silence, and not until it is over does he wish the family a Happy New Year.

December 31st   Comrie,
Flambeaux Procession   Perthshire, Scotland

Here one of the most exciting Hogmanay celebrations takes place. Townspeople in fancy dress, led by pipers and torch-bearers, march to the main square. There the costumes are judged and prizes given. Dancing, singing and general merry-making follow, and the revels come to an end when the torches have burned out.

December 31st   Stonehaven,
Swinging the Fireballs   Kincardineshire, Scotland

Swinging the fireballs is a fishermen's custom, a relic, no doubt, of a Druidic fire ritual. Balls of wire-netting filled with ropes and rags soaked in paraffin have been prepared, and when the clock strikes twelve they are set alight by young men who parade through the town swinging them round their heads from a long wire. When they reach the High Street they release the fireballs in flaming arcs.

Christmas

IN one sense Christmas never had a beginning. A kind of 'Christmas' was celebrated thousands of years before Jesus was born. In Mesopotamia, 2000 B.C., people welcomed their New Year with a twelve-day festival. There were plays, processions and merry-making, bright fires and present-giving. The people were worshipping Marduk, a god who had a yearly struggle with the monsters of chaos that lurked in underground regions. In other words, winter was dying and the New Year was being born.

Civilisation began in the East, and the customs and beliefs of early men gradually spread to the north and west of Europe. In those primitive societies the year was full of festivals, and most of them were connected with the sun and the earth, the growing and ripening of crops and the change of the seasons.

In winter the hours of daylight were few, the sun was weak, and life seemed at a standstill. Men's minds turned to thoughts of death and decay. They therefore tried to encourage what they thought was the dying sun to new life by lighting bonfires, so that the world would not be left without light and warmth. They tried to show the seeds in the ground that there was life even in the dead season by hanging evergreens on their buildings. When the days began to lengthen and the sun grew stronger, and when seeds and plants began to grow, they believed that their fires and evergreens had brought about a miracle. So the next year they repeated the process, and every year afterwards. The customs of primitive peoples resembled each other very closely, so this kind of thing was happening all over Europe in those far-off days.

In time the Winter Solstice celebrations were replaced by the festival of the Saturnalia, which was at its height during the years of the Roman Empire.

Saturn was the god of agriculture. In Roman mythology he was overthrown by Jupiter. The festival to commemorate this legendary happening began about the middle of December and continued until the Kalends of January ushered in the New Year. December 25th, the day when the sun was at its lowest and weakest, was thus the turning point of the year. It was called *Dies Natalis Invicti Solis*—the Birthday of the Unconquered Sun.

At the same time, the barbarians of the north of Europe were keeping a similar winter festival known as the Yule. Great logs were set ablaze in honour of their gods Odin and Thor, and people clustered round the bonfires, drinking from horns filled with mead and listening to their poets and minstrels singing ancient songs and legends. Mistletoe was ceremoniously cut, and sacrifices were made to mark the turn of the year.

The Yule log was burned at Christmas even up to quite recent times. In many homes a huge log was chosen from a forest tree, dragged home and decorated with greenery and ribbons. After it had dried it was burned, and any parts that had not burned away at the end of the twelve days were kept till the following year so that the new log could be kindled with wood from the old one. It could only be lit by someone with clean hands.

The Yule log had, it was believed, a magical effect in helping the sun to shine more brightly, but the cheerful warmth it gave on dark evenings accounts for the long life of the old custom.

In Persia fires were lit to Mithras, the god who represented the light of day and the bright heavens. Later he became the god of purity and wisdom. At one time Mithraism, which was spread by soldiers who travelled about Europe, was a serious rival to Christianity.

The Saturnalia was both a gigantic fair and a festival of the home. Riotous merry-making took place in the cities and villages of the Roman Empire. The halls of houses were decked with boughs of laurels and green trees, and lamps were kept burning to protect the inhabitants from the spirits of darkness. Schools were closed during the festival, the army rested from its manœuvres, and the criminal was safe from execution. Friends visited each other, taking with them good luck presents: fruits, cakes, wax candles, clay dolls, articles of gold and silver, and grains of frankincense.

Masters feasted with their slaves, who were given the freedom to do and say what they liked. They could also wear a pointed hat, which was normally the head-dress that only freemen could wear. A Mock King, representing Saturn, was appointed to take charge of the revels, and his word was law as long as his reign lasted. The wilder his antics and the more impudent his words, the louder he was cheered. (In the Christmas festivities of the Middle Ages in England the Lord of Misrule was allowed a similar licence.)

Processions in the streets were made up of people with blackened faces or wearing masks, dressed in animal skins. As no one could recognise the person behind the mask there was a good deal of horseplay, and some people looked on the yearly festival as a vulgar affair. The hats we find in our Christmas crackers are a reminder of the fantastic headpieces the Romans wore during their Saturnalia, and the black faces and animal skins are perpetuated in mummers' plays.

All these old pagan customs, however, interesting and important as they were, might in time have died out completely had it not been for the birth of Jesus, nearly two thousand years ago.

Jesus was born when Herod was the puppet king of Galilee, and that is about as near as we can get to the exact time of his birth. The custom of reckoning dates from his birth was not started until A.D. 533. Before then, years had been counted from the foundation of Rome in 753 B.C. A Russian monk named Dionysius introduced the Christian calendar, but unfortunately he made a mistake of at least four years in his calculations. We know that Herod died within a few days of April 1st in the year we now call 4 B.C., and as Jesus was then between six months and three years old he must have been born between 7 B.C. and 4 B.C.

The Gospel stories of Matthew and Luke describe the birth of Jesus but they do not mention any month or year. The writers were not scientists or historians, and the earliest Christians were not interested in the date of birth.

By the third century various times, from December to April, were celebrated as Christmas. January 6th was the most favoured day because it was supposed to be the day on which Jesus was baptised, and people thought that such an event would take place on the anniversary of his birth. In some eastern parts of Europe January 6th is still Christmas Day. December 25th was first adopted in Rome between 336 and 353, and gradually almost the entire Christian Church agreed to that date, which coincided with the Winter Solstice, the Yule and the Saturnalia. Another influence was the Jewish feast of the Dedication of the Temple, the 'Feast of Lights', held on December 20th or 21st, and which had originally been connected with the Winter Solstice.

The battle between the God of the Christians and the pagan gods went on for hundreds of years, but finally the latters' grip was broken. Many pagan Romans became Christians, but the Saturnalia remained. The leaders of the Christian Church decided not to try to abolish pagan festivals altogether, but to change them into Christian festivals by giving them a religious meaning. Thus the merry side of Christmas comes largely from the Saturnalia and other festivals, and the sacred side was added when the Church took over. What Christians could not abolish they rescued and adapted for their own purposes.

Eventually Christmas became such an important feast that from the fifth century to the tenth it marked the beginning of the Church's year. In 425 the Emperor Theodosius stopped all cruel circus games on Christmas Day. In 529 Justinian declared the day to be a public holiday. In 567 the leaders of the Church proclaimed that the twelve days from December 25th to January 6th, the Feast of the Epiphany, were both a festive and a sacred season.

Christianity was firmly established when the Roman Empire came to an end, destroyed by barbarian hordes from northern Europe, Germany, Hungary and Finland. The defenders of the Roman cities were defeated and scattered. There was destruction and chaos. Rome died, but the Christian Church lived on, grew and flourished. St. Augustine brought Christianity to England, St. Patrick to Ireland. In Germany St. Boniface is remembered, in Switzerland St. Columban, in Scandinavia St. Ansgar. Further east such missionaries as St. Cyril, St. Methodius and St. Adalbert spread the gospel.

On Christmas Day in 598 St. Augustine baptised more than ten thousand people in Britain.

By about the year 1100 all the nations of Europe had accepted Christianity and Christmas celebrations. For the next five hundred years the season was the peak of the year in churches, monasteries and private homes.

Christmas in the Middle Ages

In the Middle Ages the highlight of the Christmas festivities was feasting. In Tudor times the Christmas dinner began about midday and often lasted for eight or nine hours. The Lord of the Manor, surrounded by family, friends and attendants, sat on a raised platform at the end of the hall, and the huge plates of food were carried in to the blast of a trumpet. The greatest fanfare was reserved for the boar's head, which was taken in by

(*left*) Bringing in the Christmas pudding

Plate 13

(*below*) Wassailing at Tending, Hailsham, Sussex

Tar Burning
on New Year's
Eve at
Allendale,
Northumber-
land

Plate 14

Plate 15

Up-Helly-Aa',
Lerwick, Shet-
land Isles

Flambeaux Procession at Comrie, Perthshire

Plate 16

Lighting the torches at the Flambeaux Celebrations at Comrie, Perthshire

the chief cook. The whole company rose to their feet and gazed with awe at the sight. The head looked so lifelike, with sprigs of rosemary sticking out of its ears and an apple or orange in its mouth. The rosemary represented the returning summer and the fruit the sun. In ancient times the boar was associated with Frey, the Norse goddess of fertility, and was sacrificed to her.

Other dishes included swan, partridge, larks, venison, boiled capon and roast goose. But next in importance to the boar was the peacock, the preparation of which was a very skilled job. First the skin, with the feathers intact, was stripped off, and when the bird had been roasted the skin was slipped back and sewn on. The beak was painted with gold leaf, and a piece of cotton, soaked in spirit and set alight, was put in the mouth. This dish was considered too important for a servant to serve and it was carried to the table by the most distinguished women guests.

The table was laden with bowls of fruit, hot pies, bowls of ale with toasted apples bobbing about in them, and sugary sweets shaped into ships and castles. While the meal was in progress jesters and musicians pranced and danced about the hall and mummers in masks paraded up and down. The Lord of Misrule, a bald-headed, red-nosed clown, was there too, cracking jokes and lording it over the feast.

In poorer homes there was nothing like such a gigantic feast, but every family managed to have a large bird at Christmas, goose, capon, bustard or chicken. Turkeys were unknown until the beginning of the sixteenth century when they were introduced from Mexico. Great flocks of turkeys were reared in Norfolk and Suffolk, and just before Christmas they were driven to London, grazing on the wayside verges on the way.

Mince pies were eaten in England long before they became particularly associated with Christmas. Crusaders returning from the Holy Land brought many new things back with them, among them spices—cinnamon, ginger, cloves and nutmegs. These were mixed with minced meat, seasoned with pepper, salt and vinegar and covered by a pastry crust. Before the Reformation the mince pie was oblong, to represent a manger. Often there was a little figure of the baby Jesus on top. This ved when the 'manger' was eaten. When the Puritans forbade all Christmas activities, mince pies had to disappear, though people still ate them in secret.

By the end of the seventeenth century the character of the mince pie had changed. In addition to chopped chicken or beef tongue, it contained eggs, raisins, orange and lemon peel, sugar and spices. Then the meat part gradually disappeared, and the pie as we know it came into being, circular and without its figure of Jesus. To ensure a happy year one had to eat a mince pie on each of the Twelve Days of Christmas and say 'Happy month' before taking the first bite.

Plum porridge was also a popular dish at Christmas. It really was a porridge, a mixture of raisins and spices, bread-crumbs and fruit juices. It was served with the first course of the Christmas dinner and as it was in a semi-liquid state had to be eaten with a spoon. It did not become the pudding we know until about 1670. The custom of stirring the pudding and wishing is a very old one, and some people still put a silver coin, a ring and a thimble in the mixture. Finding the coin brings good fortune, the ring means a wedding and the thimble stands for a happy but unmarried life.

In England the Christmas drink was the wassail, which was always served in a large bowl made of apple wood. It consisted of ale, roast apples, eggs, sugar, nutmegs, cloves and ginger, and was drunk while hot. 'Wassail' comes from two old Saxon words, *Was haile*, meaning 'Your health'. Wassailing came to mean any kind of Christmas revels where a lot of drinking was done. In the eighteenth century wassail gave way to punch, which contains stronger spirits.

In Victorian times the wassail bowl was still carried from door to door in country places. In answer to the song of the wassailers: 'Wassail! Wassail! All over the town, our toast it is white, our ale it is brown', neighbours would fill the bowl with ale or cider to make sure of a good apple harvest the next autumn. The tradition, a relic of prehistoric tree worship, was much older than Christmas.

Christmas Entertainments

For over eight hundred years one of the regular Christmas entertainments was mumming. Young men and girls would dress up, sometimes in each other's clothes, sometimes wearing masks, and would give a display of dancing and a play at various houses, expecting in return a gift of money or food. These performances were for common people, not the high-born, and were not intended for the stage.

The mummers' play was performed year after year, without a break, in all parts of the country. The words were never written down, but were passed on from one generation to another so that in time there were many variations of the dialogue and action, though the central theme remained the same. Good defeated evil. St. George killed the dragon or the Turkish Knight (a hint that the Crusades were involved in the development of the play). But the play is so old that its beginnings cannot be traced, though evidently they are to be found in primitive pagan rites which were designed to soothe the forces of nature. The play was certainly connected with the festivals of the Winter Solstice and the Vernal Equinox (Christmas and Easter), and these seasons are still the seasons of the mummers' play.

The play usually began with a sword dance in which a mock death and resurrection were danced. The victim stood or knelt in the centre of a ring and the rest of the dancers locked their swords round his neck. The swords were drawn and the victim fell 'dead'. Thus died the spirit of life or the old year. Then followed a dance of rejoicing when the swords were withdrawn, the victim came to life again, just as life is renewed in the spring.

During the fifteenth century the dance expanded into a crude play, with dialogue in rhyming couplets, and there has been little change in the play since then. The chief incident is a fight which brings the hero to the point of death. He is restored to life by a doctor who claims to cure 'Ipsy, pipsy, palsy and gout, pains within and pains without'—a reminder of the early medicine man. At the end of the play there is clowning and gaiety in which all the characters join. The hero might be St.

George, Robin Hood, or another hero from legend or ballad. Often there were male and female clowns named Tommy and Bessy. Beelzebub, the Devil, was also prominent. 'Here comes I, Beelzebub, and in me hand I carries me club!'

During the reign of Henry VIII the wearing of masks was forbidden because thieves and rogues used to put them on and mix with the mummers and merrymakers.

The first Monday after January 6th was Plough Monday. The Twelve Days were over and it was time to start work on the farm. The young men decorated their ploughs and dragged them through the village. In Yorkshire and Lincolnshire they

blacked their faces, put on ribbons and masks, and went from house to house, cracking whips, singing, performing their sword dances and the Plough Monday play, which is very similar to the Christmas mumming play. The ploughboys did not realise that the idea behind their activities was to draw evil spirits from the ground where new crops were to be sown; that is what their ancestors had been doing.

Even today the plough is blessed in many churches on Plough

Monday. Farmers and farmworkers stand around the plough while the vicar blesses it, the men who use it, and the work that is to be done on the farm during the year.

Plays about the Nativity were part of Miracle Plays, which were popular between the thirteenth and sixteenth centuries, and which were originally performed in a simple way as part of a church service. Miracle Plays were based on stories taken from both the Old and New Testaments. By the fourteenth century the simple, child-like scenes had developed into longer, more elaborate plays which could be performed outside the church.

The authors were monks and the actors were members of the Craft Guilds. Each town had its own series of plays—there might be forty short plays in a play cycle—telling the whole Bible story from the Creation of the World to the Day of Judgement. Each guild in the town was responsible for one play, which was acted on a two-decker wagon in the town square or market-place. The wagons, which had dressing-rooms underneath, were rolled through the streets so that the various scenes could be presented all over the town.

The plays often started in the early morning and went on until dusk, and it might take two or three days to get through the whole cycle. They contained much rough humour. Noah's wife, for instance, was portrayed as a quarrelsome old woman, and the Devil was a bit of a clown.

The Reformation checked the popularity of Miracle Plays, and though they continued to be performed from time to time until the end of the sixteenth century, they gradually gave way to another kind of play.

This was the Morality Play which was not concerned only with Bible stories, but with the behaviour of men and women in this life. Their vices and virtues became actors on the stage, each trying in turn to influence the hero and fight for possession of his soul. From simple beginnings Morality Plays became more and more elaborate, and the number of characters increased. One of the best is *Everyman*, which was written about 1495. It is in rough but lively verse, often humorous, and with an interesting plot.

The next development was the formation of small groups of actors who performed for money and had no other work. They introduced a new kind of play, the Interlude, which was similar to the Morality Play but had no religious side. In the sixteenth century Interludes were short, comic pieces, written in simple verse, and only four or five actors were needed for their performance in banqueting halls and inn courtyards.

Up to Stuart times Christmas in London was the season of the Masque, a play in verse which included pageantry and was elaborately dressed. Ben Jonson, the famous dramatist of the seventeenth century, wrote Masques and members of the royal family often took part in them. Inigo Jones designed the dresses.

It was not until the nineteenth century that the Nativity play came into its own again. Those we see nowadays have nothing in common with Masques or Morality Plays, but are much more like the plays of earlier times—those which told the Christmas story with simple devotion and without fuss.

Pantomime was a form of entertainment that arose in the eighteenth century and has lasted until our own times. It is an entirely British institution. No other nation has ever imitated it successfully, though it still retains a connection with its continental beginnings.

In 1717 John Rich produced a pantomime called *Harlequin Executed* in a theatre in Lincoln's Inn Fields in London. There were two parts to it, one dramatic, the other comic. The first part was a fairy-tale story enacted in a straightforward way, followed by a transformation. The Fairy Queen turned the fairy-tale characters into the characters of the Harlequinade, and there developed the comic story of the courtship of Harlequin and Columbine. A family of clowns, the Grimaldis, came to England in 1758, and the comedy of pantomime became more important than the drama and scenic effects.

John Rich produced one pantomime after another for forty-five years, and all were highly successful. The pattern of pantomime has changed little since his day. The Harlequinade has died out, but the fairy story or nursery rhyme still provides a thin plot, and a magnificent transformation scene is the highlight of the performance.

Some of the games played at Christmas have a very ancient history. Blindman's Buff was played in the Middle Ages, and so was Nuts in May. Crackers and indoor fireworks remind us of the ancient fire-games that were popular; paper hats and charades take us back to the Saturnalia.

There are some games that children played, however, that have not lasted. Today we only know the names of such games as 'Feed the Dove', 'Rowland Bo', 'Shoeing the Wild Mare' and 'The Parson has lost his Cloak'.

Christmas Disappears

During the sixteenth century a number of European countries were influenced by the Reformation. Many Christians broke away from the Catholic Church and became Protestants. Religion was 'purified', and many of the old customs died out or were suppressed. The Church forbade processions, colourful ceremonies and plays, and all that remained of the old Christmas services were prayers and sermons.

The Civil War broke out in 1642. In the same year the first orders were given that Christmas festivities could no longer be held, and five years later Parliament passed a law that Christmas was to be abolished altogether. As the season approached the Mayor of every town ordered the Town Crier to warn the citizens that they were not to celebrate Christmas in any way. If they did, they were severely punished. Shops and markets stayed open and men went to work as usual. Parliament sat on every Christmas Day in order to set a good example.

Such an unpopular order could not go unchallenged, and there were riots in London, Oxford, Ipswich and Canterbury. The whole of Kent rose against the law and there were clashes between citizens and soldiers that resulted in many a broken window and many a broken head. Whole congregations were arrested and taken before the magistrates.

But slowly the light of Christmas was extinguished. December 25th became a day like any other day. Only behind closed doors was the season celebrated by people who went in constant fear of discovery.

Christmas returned when the Commonwealth gave way to

the rule of kings. With the advent of Charles II to the throne, many of the old customs were revived, but now the feasting and merry-making had a worldly rather than a religious background. Rollicking songs took the place of carols. In towns especially, the birth of Jesus was in danger of being forgotten, and the old ways lost their meaning and their popularity. By the time of Queen Anne, tournaments, masques and mummers' plays survived only in odd corners of the country where fashions changed more slowly.

Christmas Carols and Waits

For hundreds of years Christmas had no carols to add to the joys of the season. After the Reformation the old songs and carols died out and were almost forgotten until they were brought to light again in the nineteenth century, only lingering on in humble homes, remembered by people who could perhaps neither read nor write.

Carols were considered as historical relics almost to the middle of the nineteenth century. A vast number of hymns had been written during the hundred years before then, many of them by John and Charles Wesley, the founders of Methodism, and some of them, although they were not written specially for singing at Christmas, have been used for that purpose in recent years. *Hark, the herald angels sing* is one of them.

Another carol which does not strictly deserve that name is *Good King Wenceslas*, which became popular during the nineteenth century. It is really the verse-form of a medieval legend connected with St. Stephen's Day, December 26th.

Some of the best-loved carols came to us from America less than a hundred years ago. *It came upon the midnight clear, O little town of Bethlehem* and *We three kings of Orient are* all had their origin in the revival of Christmas customs across the Atlantic. *Silent Night* also comes from America, though it was first composed by an Austrian priest in 1818. The Rainers, a family of singers, took it up and made it popular all over Germany and Austria. They went on a concert tour of America in 1839, and the Americans went wild about it.

The word 'carol' comes from the Greek *choraulein. Choros*

means dance, and *aulein* means to play the flute. Ring dancing was popular with both Greeks and Romans, and it was the latter who brought the custom to Britain during their occupation two thousand years ago.

In the Middle Ages a carol was still a ring dance with a singing accompaniment. At Christmas it usually took place around a crib which had been set up inside a church. In Germany, the home of so many Christmas customs, families would dance round a baby in a cradle in the home.

The first hymns that honoured the birth of Jesus were written in the fifth century, when Christmas had been officially recognised as one of the Church's great feasts. They were written in Latin and were very solemn. St. Francis, who lived in Italy in the thirteenth century, was the first man to introduce the joyful spirit into carols, and the songs that he and other friars wrote spread from Italy to France and Spain, and thence all over Europe.

Other early carols can be found in some of the Miracle Plays. The *Coventry Carol*, for instance, comes from the Coventry Mystery Play. They resemble folk songs, as do the carols which tell a story that has only a distant connection with the Bible. *Dives and Lazarus* and *King Herod and the Cock* are two examples. There is a manuscript in Balliol College Library in Oxford which contains a collection of carols, including some from the early fifteenth century, which were written down from memory by an alderman grocer of London between the years 1500 and 1536.

During the Commonwealth many carols were preserved in folk songs or printed on broadsheets as 'matter suitable for Christmas'. They were kept hidden until the people were allowed to sing again.

In France, carols are called *Noëls*, from which word we get 'Nowell'. One of the earliest French carols commemorates the flight of Jesus, Joseph and Mary into Egypt. French carols are sparkling and gay, but those of Germany are sober and dignified. *In dulci jubilo* and *A great and mighty wonder* are two of them. German musicians were the first to introduce harmony into the tunes. Johann Sebastian Bach treated many in this way.

The largest group of carols naturally tell the story of the Nativity. Others give the shepherds' point of view and include the message of the angels and the gifts that the shepherds took to the stable. Others recount the story of the journey of the Wise Men, their adoration and their gifts, and are called Epiphany carols.

Some medieval carols describe imaginary events. *As Joseph was a-walking* is one of them. A custom which was once widespread in much of Europe at the end of the Middle Ages was the singing of 'Star' carols. These were sung by young people, pretending to be the Wise Men, as they went from house to house carrying a pole with the Star of Bethlehem on top. Today, in Holland, young men in fancy costumes meet in the village square on Christmas Eve. One of them, the Star Bearer, carries a star-shaped lantern at the head of the procession, and they wend their way through the streets, singing carols as they go.

The practice of singing round a Christmas tree set up in the open air is growing in England. Every year a huge tree from Norway is set up in Trafalgar Square in London, and crowds gather round it to sing carols.

The best-known carol service is the Festival of the Nine Lessons held in King's College Chapel, in Cambridge, on Christmas Eve. It is opened by a solo performance of *Once in Royal David's City* and is sung by a chorister who is told that he has been chosen only just before the service starts. Nine ancient carols are sung, interspersed by readings from the Gospel. The service takes place in candlelight. It was first broadcast in 1930, and is now a regular feature of radio and television.

In the Middle Ages the gates of the walled cities were guarded by watchmen called waits. One of their duties was to sound the hours, and this they did by blowing a single note or a simple tune on an instrument rather like an oboe. Some of these watchmen became good enough musicians to play on official occasions. In the early sixteenth century London's Corporation Waits wore a blue uniform with red sleeves, a red cap, a silver collar and chain of office. They played before the Mayor and Corporation at banquets and in processions. Waits still played at Bath up to the beginning of the nineteenth century.

The development of the Police Force, however, made watchmen unnecessary and gradually waits ceased to exist, though the name lived on for any group of musicians who went around playing and singing at Christmas time. They played reed or brass instruments which made a loud noise and were not affected by the weather. Their repertoire included both carols and the popular music of the day, and they expected their efforts to be rewarded by money or drinks.

Father Christmas

The legend of Father Christmas goes back over sixteen hundred years to Myra in Asia Minor, then a province of the Roman Empire. There, during the reigns of the emperors Diocletian, Maximilian and Constantine, lived a man called Nicholas. His parents were wealthy Christians and eventually he became the Bishop of Myra. He was imprisoned by Diocletian when Christians were being persecuted, and later released by Constantine the Great. He died on December 6th (now his feast day) about the year 326, and in 1087 his body was taken from Asia Minor to Bari in Italy, where his relics are kept in the Church of San Nicola.

These few facts are all that are known about St. Nicholas, but an amazing number of legends have grown up around him. His goodness, gentleness and great love of children endeared him to all. He was happy only when he was helping poor people. His presents always came as a surprise, though, for he did not like his generosity to be talked about.

By the year 1200 grown-ups and children in every country in Europe loved St. Nicholas. He became the patron saint of many towns. Hundreds of churches were dedicated to him and round the English coast alone there were nearly four hundred. He was specially revered by sailors and travellers because he was believed to ride storms at sea and save lives. Greek and Russian seamen always kept a little statue of St. Nicholas in the ship's forecastle and prayed to him when danger threatened. Dutch boats carried his statue as a figurehead on the prow. He was known to the Lapps and the fishermen of the Arctic Circle, where reindeer are common, and became also the patron saint of parish clerks, scholars and pawnbrokers.

In Norway and Germany children believe that St. Nicholas has an assistant called Kris Kringle (the name comes from *Christkind* or Christ Child) whose job is to drive the sledge over the rooftops. In Switzerland St. Nicholas has a wife named Lucy. She gives presents to the girls while her husband deals with the boys. Children in the lower Rhine valley put out clogs to be filled on the eve of December 6th and put hay in them for the saint's white horse. Their parents put out bundles of grain and sometimes a little wooden ship. In the morning the hay is gone and the clogs are filled with sweetmeats.

In Holland, Switzerland and parts of Austria and Germany the saint is represented by a man dressed as a bishop who preaches a sermon and hears the children say their catechism before giving them their presents. Dutch children say that he is accompanied by a black servant, and if they have been naughty there is some talk of them being put in the servant's sack and carried off to Spain.

The origin of Knight Rupprecht, who comes with St. Nicholas in some parts of central and northern Europe, is obscure. He probably started out as a heathen god, perhaps Odin. He wears skins or straw and looks very fierce. He makes the children say their prayers and threatens to punish them if they do not know them well enough.

Epiphany is present-giving time for Italian children, as it is in Spain. The person who brings the presents is Befana, a female spirit about whom little is known, except that she is a left-over from pre-Christian times. She warns naughty children that she will eat them up if they do not improve their behaviour.

In the seventeenth century St. Nicholas was introduced to America by the early Dutch settlers. They led him through the streets of New Amsterdam on a white horse and accompanied by a Moorish servant called Peter. The Dutch called him *Sinterklass*, and the name eventually turned into Santa Claus. The stately bishop turned into the red-faced, white-bearded old gentleman we now know as Father Christmas.

From America Father Christmas was 'exported' to England little more than a hundred years ago (a writer in 1827 referred to the American tradition as 'unknown to us') and he found a warm welcome.

In the customs and legends that have arisen around the figure of St. Nicholas there is a curious hint that Odin is somehow mixed up in it all. Odin has a history that goes back two thousand years. Sometimes he left his throne to direct the affairs of men. Barefoot, wearing a long cloak and a wide hat, he rode Sleipnir, his white horse with eight legs, or lashed his reindeer through the snow. He appeared on the eve of December 6th, when days are short but the New Year is in sight. He, too, rode the storm and saved mariners' lives. Sometimes he went hunting through the air with horsemen and hounds. Peasants in north Europe still believe they can see Odin's wild hunt in the storm.

It would seem that St. Nicholas and Odin have become the same person, that the Christian saint has inhabited the body of the Norse god, thus providing another example of Christian customs displacing those of the Yule and the Winter Solstice. It is difficult to be certain, however, because the stories are made up of so many threads from so many periods of history and from so many countries.

Christmas Evergreens

At Christmas time most houses are decorated with evergreens, chiefly holly and mistletoe, though laurel, rosemary and bay are sometimes used too. Such decorations are not brought into the house until Christmas Eve, or a few days before Christmas. They are kept up until Twelfth Night, January 6th, then taken down and burnt. In the middle of the seventeenth century Robert Herrick wrote:

> *Down with the Rosemary, and so*
> *Down with the Baies and mistletoe;*
> *Down with the Holly, Ivie, all*
> *Wherewith ye drest the Christmas Hall.*

In some places evergreens were not taken down until

, Candlemas Day.

n is another that has been borrowed from the
saturnalia when the temples dedicated to pagan gods
were decorated with evergreens. When Christianity had
spread through Europe the early Christian priests remembered
the words of Isaiah: 'The glory of Lebanon shall come unto
thee, the fir tree, the pine tree, and the box together, to beautify
the place of my sanctuary', and the practice of decorating
churches and homes with plants and flowers was allowed to
continue. In 604 Pope Gregory I wrote a letter to St. Augustine
of Canterbury in which he gave permission for them to be used
at Christmas time.

Leaves that remain green all the year round have always been
a symbol of eternal life. In addition, they are usually the only
greenery available in the middle of winter, and they are the
only bushes that bear berries.

In England sprigs of holly are very popular. The prickly
points of its leaves have always reminded people of the crown
of thorns that Jesus was forced to wear when he was crucified.
The red berries represented the drops of blood on his forehead.
In medieval times holly was believed to possess special healing
powers, and it was used to treat fevers, rheumatism and
asthma. A lost traveller would always look for a holly bush
under which to shelter and so be safe from evil spirits. Holly
inside a house was a protection against fire and storms. If a
piece of holly taken from church decorations was hung in a room
there would be happiness and holiness in that room all through
the coming year.

Mistletoe was a sacred plant in Britain long before Christianity arrived. It was used in religious festivals by most northern
peoples. The Druids worshipped the Norse gods Odin, Thor
and Baldur. Mistletoe was their holy plant, and when they used
it they were thanking the gods for the end of the dark winter
days and the coming of spring. They cut it from the tree on
which it grew with a gold-handled knife or sickle and handed it
to the people, calling it 'All-Heal'.

Like the holly, mistletoe was supposed to have miraculous
powers. It could heal almost anything, from epilepsy to tooth-

ache. This is interesting, for the Druids did not know that mistletoe contains a drug that is helpful in the treatment of nervous diseases. Their belief, therefore, was the result of experiments and was not based on theory. Mistletoe also gave protection from witchcraft and brought good luck. To hang it over a doorway or in a room was to offer goodwill to visitors. Kissing under the mistletoe was a pledge of friendship. This custom is one that is found only in England or in countries where English people have settled. It appears that at one time the English used to exchange kisses much more freely than they do now, for Erasmus, a Dutch visitor to England in the sixteenth century, wrote: 'Wherever you go everyone welcomes you with a kiss, and the same on bidding farewell . . . in short, turn where you will, there are kisses, kisses everywhere.' In some parts of the country the mistletoe was burnt after Twelfth Night as an insurance that the boys and girls who had kissed under it would indeed get married.

Because mistletoe was associated with the often cruel practices of the Druids, Christians were forbidden to hang it up in churches, and even today it is seldom seen in a sacred building.

In pre-Christian Rome the ivy was linked with Bacchus, the god of wine, and his drunken feasts, and it was banished from Christian homes when Christianity superseded paganism. The old tradition that ivy should be allowed only outside the house is still strong. On the Continent especially it is hardly ever used.

Laurel is a symbol of victory. The Greeks crowned their great men with laurel wreaths, and the Romans used laurel boughs for decoration during their festivals. The American custom of hanging a laurel wreath on the front door at Christmas time is a direct link with pagan Rome. As the bush was held in such high regard, it was fitting for the early Christians to decorate their homes with it to celebrate the birth of Jesus, and it was also much used in churches.

Rosemary has been connected with Christmas for hundreds of years. An old legend tells of Mary putting the baby Jesus's clothes on a rosemary bush to dry when the Holy Family were on their way to Egypt. The bush gave the tiny garments such a sweet smell that God honoured it for the service it had given.

s not used as a Christmas decoration as much as
stletoe are, but it still has its place in many homes.

The Christmas Tree

During the Saturnalia the Romans hung little masks of
Bacchus on pine trees. It is tempting to think that these were
the first 'Christmas' trees, but it is much more likely that the
custom of having a decorated tree at this season of the year
originated in Germany, where it is much older than in England.
There is a legend about St. Boniface, who lived in the eighth
century, that hints at a possible beginning. It is said that one
Christmas Eve he cut down an oak tree, which was sacred to the
pagans he was trying to convert, and offered them instead a
young fir tree, as a symbol of the new faith he preached. During
the Reformation, Martin Luther is said to have used a candlelit
tree to represent the starry heavens. We know that fir trees
were used at Christmas in the sixteenth century because a
writer in Strasbourg in 1605 recorded that it was the custom of
the people of that town to set up little fir trees in their best
rooms and decorate them with apples, sweets and paper roses.

There is also a connection between the fir tree and the
Mystery Plays of the Middle Ages. One popular play was the
Paradise play. The Garden of Eden was represented by a fir
tree, which was hung with apples, and the play was performed
inside a ring of lighted candles, either inside the church or just
outside it. The Paradise tree survived after the play had lapsed
into disuse, and at Christmas time it became the custom for a
fir tree to be taken into the home and decorated with small white
wafers to represent the Body of Christ, the coming Saviour.
Later the wafers were replaced by pieces of pastry cut into stars,
angels, hearts, flowers and bells. In the middle of the seventeenth century, candles and glittering decorations were added.

At first, Christmas trees were found only in the valley of the
Upper Rhine, but gradually they became popular in other parts
of Germany.

Prince Albert, the husband of Queen Victoria, is usually given
the credit of introducing the Christmas tree to England when
one was brought from his native Germany in 1841 and set up

in Windsor Castle, but actually his was not the first to be seen in this country. There was one at least twenty years before, brought over from Germany by a member of Queen Caroline's household for a children's party. Eight years later a German princess staying in England set up three Christmas trees. In 1831 a Swiss governess introduced one to her employer's house. German merchants who had settled in Manchester observed the custom, and by 1840 it was quite widespread. But it was undoubtedly the Prince Consort's tree that really took the public fancy, and by the middle of last century there were hundreds of trees for sale at Covent Garden, and a huge one was set up at the Crystal Palace.

When the Christmas tree came in, the Kissing Bough went

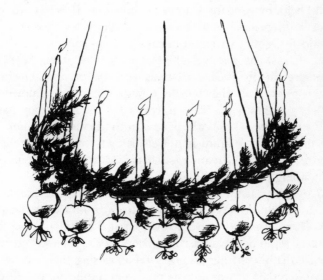

out. This was a half circle of evergreen with a ring of candles above and a ring of red apples below, and a bunch of mistletoe hanging below the apples. The framework was made either of iron or shoots of willow. Sometimes small presents were fastened to it by long ribbons. It was hung from the middle of the ceiling, like a crown, and was just high enough for two people to stand underneath it and kiss under the mistletoe.

The candles on the Kissing Bough were lit on Christmas Eve, and relit every evening until Twelfth Night. The family and their friends sang carols beneath it, mummers played under it and children danced under it. It was, in fact, the centre of the Christmas festivities, but only in Britain. Although the Christmas tree put the Kissing Bough out of favour, it lingered on in remote parts of the country, and today it may still be seen in a few farms and cottages in the north-west of England.

Christmas Cards

Christmas cards, which are now sent out in millions every year, were unknown just over a hundred years ago. The fore-runner of the card was the 'Christmas piece', which was an exercise in handwriting done by boys at school and taken home at the beginning of the Christmas holidays. It was written on paper with printed and coloured headings and borders, and contained greetings written in careful copperplate.

But Christmas pieces had disappeared by about 1856, ten years after the first real Christmas card was printed. The credit for this goes to Sir Henry Cole, though it has been claimed that in 1842 the first card was engraved by a London boy named William Egley, whose card is now in the British Museum. The date under his signature is not clear, and the last figure could be either a 2 or a 9. In any case, his effort aroused little interest and nothing came of his idea.

In 1843 Sir Henry Cole suggested to J. C. Horsley, an artist, that he should design a card about the size of a lady's visiting card. Horsley produced a hand-coloured lithograph which con-sisted of three panels in a rustic framework. The central panel showed a family sitting around a table, raising their glasses for a toast. On the left was a scene representing the phrase 'feeding the hungry', and on the right, 'clothing the naked'. Under the picture were the words 'A Merry Christmas and a Happy New Year to you'. About a thousand of these cards were produced and sold at a shilling each.

In 1862 a publisher named Goodall began to print cards commercially, and on many of them the robin figured promi-nently. The robin, being a sacred bird, has long had a connection with Christmas.

Christmas cards became very popular about 1870, and during the next ten years grew very elaborate. Some were shaped like fans, stars or half moons, some were frosted or studded with 'jewels'; others were made of silk, satin or even porcelain, and were hand-painted.

Christmas Legends

Many of the legends and superstitions which surround the Christmas season must have been preserved, in a half-understood way, for thousands of years. People once believed that every living creature, birds and animals as well as human beings, shared in the joy of Jesus's birth. According to legend the raven was the first bird to know what had happened because he was flying over the place where the shepherds were guarding their sheep when they heard the good news proclaimed by the angels. The cockerel, though, was the first to tell the world, crying hoarsely, *Christus natus est* (Christ is born)—a cry that cocks have repeated ever since all through the night before Christmas Day. The wren is one of God's favoured birds because she took feathers and moss in her beak to make a covering for the baby in the manger. The cow warmed him with her breath, and as a reward has been given sweeter breath than any other animal.

In the tenth century it was thought that all the trees in the forest bloomed and bore fruit on Christmas Eve, even though the ground might be covered with frost and snow. Another story relates how the shepherds took gifts to the baby. One gave him a lambkin, another a whistle, another a small drum. But one shepherd had nothing to give, so he picked a daisy and put it to the baby's lips. Immediately the edges of the petals were stained with red, and that is the reason why many daisies still have rose-tipped petals.

Cattle turn to the east at midnight on Christmas Eve and bow; a dog which howls at that time should be shot at once for otherwise it will go mad before the New Year is out; bees hum the Hundredth Psalm in their hives; farm animals speak to each other, though it is unlucky to try and overhear what they say.

If you sit under a pine tree, you will hear the angels sing, but you will pay for it by dying early.

There is a tradition that St. Joseph of Arimathaea, a member of the Sanhedrin and secret follower of Jesus, who provided the tomb for the body of Jesus, came to Britain to preach the Gospel. On a hill near Glastonbury, aptly named Weary-all Hill, he thrust his staff of thornwood into the ground. The staff took root and grew into a tree which blossomed twice a year, once on Christmas Eve and again in the spring. When the calendar was changed in 1752, September 2nd became September 14th, and England 'lost' eleven days. The Christmas festival, therefore, arrived eleven days earlier, and has done ever since. But many people resisted the change. 'Give us back our eleven days!' they cried. They watched the Glastonbury Thorn to see whether it would flower on the old date, now January 5th, or on the new Christmas Eve, and when it ignored the new calendar they considered that there had been wicked interference with the date of the Nativity.

During the Commonwealth, soldiers cut down the tree, leaving only the stump, but cuttings were taken and planted in other places, including the grounds of Glastonbury Abbey. The Abbey is now in ruins, but the thorn tree still grows bravely. Many people still visit the trees on the night of January 5th, hoping to see the buds break into flower. Sometimes their patience is rewarded because the hawthorns at Glastonbury belong to a variety which *does* blossom twice a year, in the winter if the season is mild, and in the spring.

Boxing Day

December 26th is the Feast of Stephen, the first Christian martyr. It is also Boxing Day. The origin of the name is not clear, though the most likely explanation is that it comes from medieval times, when priests emptied the alms boxes which were kept in churches and gave the money to the poor of the parish the day after Christmas. Servants and apprentices had their own personal boxes in which they put the money they had received as gifts and tips during the year. As more money was given at Christmas than at any other time the opening of the boxes was delayed until the next day, when no further contributions were expected. This custom was called 'boxing'. Each present was therefore a 'box', and the day of opening the box became known as 'Boxing Day'.

Until quite recently December 26th was the day for giving money to the dustman, postman and paper boy. Clergymen were once expected to provide bread and beer and cheese for their parishioners, and farm labourers received pies that the farmer's wife had baked.

In Scotland Handsel Monday, the first Monday of the New Year, was the day when apprentices, journeymen and lamplighters received their boxes.

Although there is nothing in the story of St. Stephen to connect him with horses, tradition has brought the saint and the animal together, probably due to a Swedish St. Stephen, who loved horses, being confused with the martyr. It was often the custom for horse races to be run on December 26th in some northern European countries, and in England a meet is often held on Boxing Day in those counties where fox-hunting is popular.

January to April

January 6th (Plough Monday and Old Christmas Day)
Hood Game   Haxey, Lincolnshire

The legend attached to the Haxey Hood Game tells how Lady de Mowbray, the wife of a local landowner in the thirteenth century, was riding to church one Christmas Day when a fierce wind blew her scarlet hood from her head. Thirteen men who saw the incident dashed forward to pick it up, and Lady de Mowbray was so impressed by their gallantry that in her will she left a piece of land, still called the Hoodland, to the village, and gave instructions that from the rent it yielded a hood should be provided each year and that a contest for it should take place between twelve villagers dressed in scarlet jerkins and caps.

Nowadays the contest is played for twelve rolled-up pieces of canvas and one made of leather. A 'King' and a committee of twelve are responsible for the preparations.

The venue is Haxey Church Green where the people of the five parishes of Haxey gather about midday on January 6th. At 2 p.m. the church bells peal to announce the arrival of the King Boggan and his attendants. The King carries thirteen willow wands tied together with thirteen bands of willow, and his tall hat is decorated with red flowers. His twelve attendants also wear tall hats and with the party is a black-faced Fool in a patchwork costume with paper streamers hanging down his back.

The Fool recounts the story of Lady de Mowbray and her scarlet hood from the base of an old stone, all that is left of the village cross, and reminds his audience of the rules of the game. While he is speaking the paper streamers on his back are set alight and a pile of damp straw and paper is lit at his feet. 'Smoking the Fool' suggests that the ceremony has its origin in a ritual animal or human sacrifice which is, of course, far older than the legend of Lady de Mowbray. Her story may have been added later to rationalise the tradition.

The Fool is only smoked, not burned alive, fortunately, and the fire is put out before any damage is done. The Boggans lead the way to the top of Haxey Hill, and at a point on the parish boundary they form a circle of about a hundred yards radius round the King. The village people surround the circle.

The King Boggan throws up the first hood, and whoever catches it gets a shilling if he can reach the nearest inn without being tackled by a Boggan. If he is caught the hood is thrown again.

When the twelve hoods have been thrown, the leather hood is brought into play. Three rival teams try to force it into one of the three village inns, and the game turns into a huge scrum with, sometimes, hundreds of people involved. The scrum sways and heaves its way down the hill to the inns, and when someone manages to get the hood inside the inn door the game is over and there are free drinks all round. The hood is kept in the inn until the next Hood Game.

'Hoose agen hoose, toone agen toone. If thou meets a man, knock 'im down but don't hurt 'im,' says the Fool at the end of his speech, and it is remarkable that the wild scramble for the thirteenth hood has produced no serious accident.

Thursday after Plough Monday   Bury St. Edmunds,
Cakes and Ale Ceremony   Suffolk

The oldest endowed sermon is preached in St. Mary's Church on the Thursday after Plough Monday. Jankyn Smith, an eighteenth-century benefactor, built almshouses and the two chancel aisles in the church, among other bequests; and in his will he directed that his memory should be kept green by an

In addition to the sermon there is a distribution ___ ___ ___ he needy of the parish. It is traditional that the ...ng is given to the verger of the church.

Thomas Bright, another of the town's benefactors, gave a sum of money for cakes and ale to be provided at the service. Sherry has now replaced ale, and the refreshments are partaken by the Guildhall Feoffement Trustees, who are responsible for the ceremony.

January 12th (Old New Year's Eve)	Burghead,
Burning the Clavie	Morayshire, Scotland

Burghead is a seaport town with fishing as the main occupation of the people. The clavie is a tar barrel cut into two unequal parts. The larger part is broken up and the pieces are put into the smaller part. Wood chips and tar are added, then the clavie is fixed to a strong pole. None of the materials or tools used in its manufacture must be bought; so the key nail is made by a local smith, and a stone is used instead of a hammer.

At twilight the Clavie King lights the clavie with burning peat and it is paraded round the harbour and through the streets. The procession halts at the houses of the more important townspeople and a piece of the clavie is thrown through the door, in order to bring luck to the inhabitants. The clavie is then taken to a headland and becomes the base of a huge bonfire, to which broken-up casks are added.

The burning clavie is eventually rolled down the hill, and onlookers try to get a piece to take home and kindle a special New Year fire, so that witches and evil spirits will keep their distance and do no harm, at least for a year.

The origin of the celebration is in dispute. Some people believe that it is a survival of a Roman custom (there is the site of a ruined Roman temple on the headland); some that it has a Scandinavian background; others attribute it to the Druids.

January 17th (Old Twelfth Night)	Carhampton,
Wassailing the Apple Trees	Somerset

The object of this ceremony, with its undoubtedly pagan

origins, is to drive away evil spirits from the cider apple orchards, and to encourage the trees to bear good crops in the coming year. The ceremony is still observed in some parts of the country. At Carhampton, in the early evening of January 17th, the village people, and a crowd of sightseers, form a circle round the largest apple tree. The men fire guns through the branches; they throw cider over its trunk, and put pieces of toast and cake soaked in cider in the forks of the branches. This is done to thank the gods of the trees in advance for protecting their dwelling-place. Then, standing round the trees, those taking part sing the old wassail song, and a toast is drunk in cider.

Last Tuesday in January	Lerwick,
Up-Helly-Aa'	Shetland Isles

This picturesque ceremony, the climax of which is the burning of a Norse galley, dates back to Viking times, when the bodies of dead chieftains were sent to Valhalla in a blazing ship. The date chosen is the last day of the Yuletide festivities that were held during the Norse occupation of Scotland to celebrate the triumph of the sun over the darkness of winter.

The commander of the day's proceedings, which have taken at least a month to prepare, is the Chief Guiser, and he has over three hundred Guisers, divided into groups of eight or ten, in his command. A thirty-foot model of a Viking ship, with

dragon's head bow, is paraded through the streets and taken towards the sea. Its crew wear Viking dress and are accompanied by the Guisers. From its gunwales protrude oars with shields bearing heraldic devices above them, and a banner flies from the masthead.

After dark the galley leads a huge torchlight procession to the sea. The bands play *The Galley Song*; maroons are fired from the fort and rocket salvoes are released from the ships in the harbour. The tune changes to *The Norseman's Home* as torches are flung into the galley, which is soon a flaming mass as it goes to its Valhalla.

The revelry that follows lasts well into the night.

January 31st   Guildford,
Dicing for the Maid's Money   Surrey

John How, a citizen of Guildford who died in 1674, left £400 in his will with instructions that two maidservants should dice for the interest of £11 19s. He stipulated that the two maids should not be employed in a beerhouse or hostelry. The contest takes place annually at the Guildhall.

The winner takes all the money, but the loser actually comes off better financially. This topsy-turvy state of affairs comes about because in 1702 John Parsons, another benefactor, left £600 to be invested and the interest given every year to 'a poor young man' who had served a seven-year apprenticeship in the town. When, after a long period, no suitable applicant could be found, it was decided that the interest on John Parson's bequest should go to the loser of the Maid's Money contest. As the amount is a few pence greater, the loser gains more!

February 2nd (or the Sunday nearest the Feast
of the Purification of the Blessed Virgin Mary)   Blidworth,
Cradle Rocking   Nottinghamshire

This ceremony is a re-acting of the Presentation of Christ in the Temple, and used to appear in the Miracle Plays of the Middle Ages. It was revived at St. Mary's Church, Blidworth, in 1922.

The last boy child in the parish who has been baptised before the Feast of the Purification is placed in an old wooden cradle on rockers which stands before the altar. After a short re-dedication service the vicar rocks the cradle about twelve times and then hands the child back to his parents while the *Nunc dimittis* is sung.

First Monday in February   St. Ives,
Hurling the Silver Ball   Cornwall

The patron saint of St. Ives is St. Ia, and Feasten Day is the day after the Feast of St. Ia. The highlight of the day is the playing of a ball game which resembles 'Passing the Parcel', but which is played, chiefly by children, with a ball about the size of a tennis ball. It is made of light wood and is covered with silver leaf.

At 10.30 a.m. the Mayor of St. Ives throws the ball against the wall of the parish church, from which it bounces back into the crowd. Then it is tossed from hand to hand. The game, which used to be played in the streets, then on the beach, is now played in a public park. It goes on until midday, and whoever has possession of the ball when the church clock begins to chime receives a reward of 25 pence. The ball is returned to the Mayor for use the following year.

In the afternoon there are sports, and in the evening the Town Ball is held.

The first Tuesday after the new moon
following February 2nd (Candlemas)   Jedburgh,
Fastern E'en Ba'   Roxburghshire, Scotland

Candlemas Day is celebrated at Jedburgh by a strange kind of football game played between the Uppies (those born on the north side of the market cross) and the Downies (those born on the south side). The game begins in the early afternoon, and continues through the day. Several leather balls with streamers attached are used as they frequently disappear. The streets of the town and the River Jed constitute the pitch; a goal area is chosen at each end of the town, one at Castle Hill, the other at the Town foot, and the player who, after much struggling and pushing, gets the ball into the goal receives a cash award.

The game arouses great enthusiasm in the town; all work stops, schools close for the day, and shopkeepers barricade their windows.

The ball is said to represent an Englishman's head, and the origin of the game is likely to lie in a long-ago battle between the English and the Scots at Fernieherst Castle, after which the winners (the Scots) hacked off the heads of their enemies and kicked them around in triumph.

Shrovetide

Shrovetide covers the last three or four days before the beginning of Lent. The old names for these days were Egg Saturday, Quinquagesima Sunday, Collop Monday and Shrove Tuesday. When Lent was observed more rigorously than it is now, Shrovetide was celebrated by games, sports, dancing and other revelries. There were feasts to use up the food that could not be eaten during the Lenten fast. Football was played in the streets and Nickanan Night (as Shrove Monday evening was called in Cornwall) was a time for boys to run riot in the villages: hiding gates, taking off door knockers, and making off with anything that householders had forgotten to lock away.

The Monday evening was also called Lent-sherd Night or Dappy-door Night. Children went round the village in twos and threes chanting a verse, hoping to be given cakes, eggs, flour, butter or money as contributions to the following day's feast. In Devon they sang:

> *I see by the latch*
> *There is something to catch;*
> *I see by the string*
> *The good dame's within;*
> *Give a cake, for I've none;*
> *At the door goes a stone,*
> *Come give, and I've gone.*

Sometimes the doors of unpopular villagers were battered by a shower of broken crockery and earthenware, the children singing as they threw:

> *Skit, scat,*

Take this and take that.

Dappy-doorers would ring bells or knock loudly on doors and run off quickly before the summons could be answered. One of their favourite tricks was to tie a long piece of string to a door handle, knock at the door and then hide round a corner. When the householder opened the door the string was given a sudden pull, and the astonished man would find the handle jerked violently from his grasp.

Shrovetide was also the time for hurling matches, cock-fighting, wrestling and horse-racing—anything, in fact, that would give opportunities for exercise and the release of energy before the solemnity of Lent put an end to such things. Good people prepared for the fast by going to church to confess their sins and be shriven, but most people concerned themselves with merry-making, practical jokes and over-eating.

On Collop Monday bacon, eggs and fried collops of meat were eaten, and on Shrove Tuesday fats and butter were used up in the making of pancakes.

Shrove Tuesday (a movable feast between
February 2nd and March 8th)   Olney,
Pancake Day Race   Buckinghamshire

'Shrove' comes from the old Roman Catholic practice of confessing sins and being shriven or shrove—that is, obtaining absolution. This was carried out on Ash Wednesday, the first day of Lent. The fact that we eat pancakes on Shrove Tuesday is because housewives had to use up their stocks of fat, butter and eggs, foods which were forbidden during Lent.

The annual Pancake Race at Olney is one of the most popular of current Shrove Tuesday customs, and is said to be more than five hundred years old. According to tradition, in 1445 a woman of Olney heard the shriving bell while she was making pancakes and ran to church in her apron, still clutching her frying-pan.

Only women may take part in the race. The Pancake Bell is rung at 11.30 a.m. and again at 11.45 to warn contestants to get ready, and at 11.55 the race, which is over a 415-yard-long course, begins.

Each contestant has a frying-pan containing a pancake which is still cooking. She must toss the pancake three times during the race, which starts from the market square, and the first woman to reach the church door and serve her pancake to the bellringer receives a kiss from him. She and the runner-up also receive a prayer book from the vicar. Those taking part must wear an apron and a hat or scarf; slacks are forbidden.

A similar race takes place at the same time in Liberal, Kansas, in the U.S.A., and since 1950 there has been friendly rivalry between the two towns to record the fastest time. Liberal rings up Olney immediately after the race to give their result and hear Olney's.

Bodiam in Sussex and North Somercotes in Lincolnshire also hold a Pancake Race, but neither attracts the number of visitors nor receives the publicity that Olney does.

Shrove Tuesday	Westminster School,
Pancake Greaze	London

Tossing the pancake is observed with great ceremony at Westminster School. At 11 a.m. a verger of Westminster Abbey leads a procession into the school. The school cook tosses a huge pancake over a 16-feet-high bar which separates the Upper School from the Lower School, and the boys scramble for it. The boy who emerges from the scrum with the largest piece of pancake receives a cash reward, as does the cook.

A former practice of the boys, abandoned over a hundred years ago, was to throw books at the cook if he failed to toss the pancake over the bar.

Shrove Tuesday	Ashbourne,
Shrovetide Football Match	Derbyshire

Games of football were played annually on Shrove Tuesday in many places in medieval times, though the earliest record we have of one was at Chester in 1553. The origin of such games is uncertain, but it is possible that in pre-Christian times men kicked around the head of an animal that had been slaughtered for a ritual sacrifice.

Before the end of the eighteenth century authority was trying to suppress the custom on the grounds that it was dangerous, disgraceful to humanity and civilisation, and destructive of morals. In most places authority won, but Ashbourne is one of the towns where the people were determined to keep up the old custom and successfully defeated all attempts to get it stopped.

The game has few rules. The Up'ards (those born north of the River Henmore which divides the town) play the Down'ards (those born south of the river), and any number may play providing they can claim to be Up'ards or Down'ards. Clifton and Sturston, three miles apart, each has a mill-wheel, and these are the goals.

The game lasts for two days and only rarely is a goal scored. This is not surprising considering the size of the pitch and the number of players involved. The game starts at 2 p.m. when a visiting celebrity throws up the ball in a field near the centre of the town, and it often continues until midnight. The River Henmore is the centre of much of the play, which is very boisterous, and the ball, which is about the size of a football, is filled with cork dust to make it heavy and the game more static.

When a goal is scored the scorer is allowed to claim the ball immediately and a replacement is brought into use. When the game begins the ball is white and has the Union Jack painted on it, but the decoration soon disappears.

Shrove Tuesday   Sedgefield,
Shrovetide Football   County Durham
The football played at Sedgefield is similar to that played at Ashbourne but does not last as long and attracts fewer spectators. The Pancake Bell is rung soon after midday to call the players together for a 1 p.m. start. As at Ashbourne, any number can take part. The ball is a small one and can be kicked greater distances than can the Ashbourne ball. The goals are half a mile apart; one is a stream, the other a pond.

Shrove Tuesday   Alnwick,
Shrovetide Football   Northumberland
At Alnwick, Shrovetide Football is played in a field which

belongs to the Duke of Northumberland, who also provides the ball and the prizes. The goals, a quarter of a mile apart, are decorated with evergreens. One of the teams is drawn from the residents of St. Michael's parish and the other from those of St. Paul's. Up to 150 players may take part.

The ball is ceremoniously taken to the field in a small procession led by the Duke of Northumberland's piper. The game is more Association than Rugby, for only the feet may be used. When three goals have been scored (each one announced by a trumpet call) the game is over. Small cash prizes are awarded to the winners of the three goals, then the ball is thrown up and scrambled for. Whoever carries it off the field is allowed to keep it.

Shrove Tuesday	Atherstone,
Shrovetide Football	Warwickshire

The contest begins at 3 p.m. and lasts for two hours. It is very much a free-for-all as women and children can join in, though they do not usually stay the full course.

The ball is filled with water so that it cannot travel more than a few yards, and it is decorated with red, white and blue ribbons. Atherstone people believe that the game began in the reign of King John, when men of Warwickshire fought with men of Leicestershire for a bag of gold.

Shrove Tuesday	Corfe Castle,
Shrovetide Football	Dorset

Here the Shrove Tuesday game has a very different origin from any of the others and is played in a very different way. The object of the game is to maintain the quarrymen's old right of way to what was once the chief harbour from which Purbeck marble was sent to Poole. There is no contest between two opposing teams; the Purbeck quarrymen just kick a football along the old road to Ower Quay. Before the game starts the Court of the Company of Marblers meets to admit new apprentices.

Plate 17
Distributing the Tichborne Dole, Hampshire

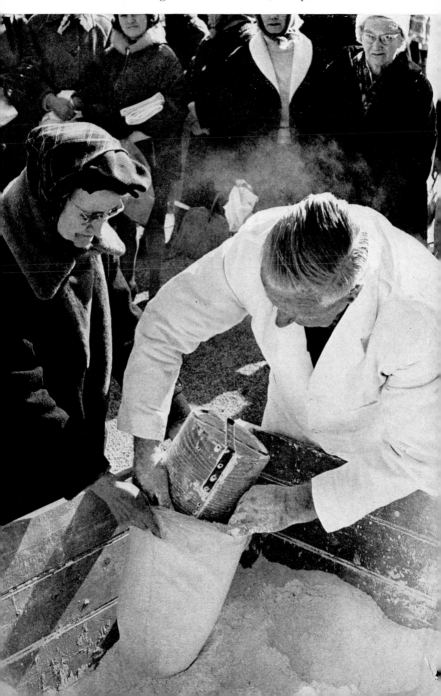

Pancake race at Olney, Buckinghamshire

Plate 18

Bottle-kicking on Easter Monday, Hallaton, Leicestershire

Hocktide Tutti-men extracting their due, with the aid of a convenient ladder, at Hungerford, Berkshire

Plate 19

The Orange Scrambler who accompanies the Tutti-men

(right) Pace-egg Play, Midgley, Yorkshire

Plate 20

(below) Nutters Dance on Easter Saturday at Bacup, Lancashire

Shrove Tuesday   St. Columb Major and
Shrovetide Hurling   St. Columb Minor, Cornwall

Hurling is an ancient Cornish sport that survives only at these two villages and at St. Ives. It is played on Shrove Tuesday and also the second Saturday after Shrove Tuesday. The game begins about 4 p.m., between two teams that may have as many as 500 a side, one the Townsmen, the other the Countrymen.

Hurling is a very vigorous affair; the ball can only be thrown, but Rugby-type tackling is allowed. The goals are a mile apart. The ball is made of wood encased in silver, and on it are inscribed the words:

> *Town and country, do your best,*
> *For in this parish I must rest.*

Shrove Tuesday   Stoke St. Gregory,
Egg-shackling   Somerset

Egg-shackling is probably a survival of an ancient seasonal ritual performed to promote fertility. It is carried on nowadays only at Stoke St. Gregory and Shepton Beauchamp. The children of these two villages take their eggs to school, each egg with its owner's name written on it. There they are 'shackled' in a sieve; that is, shaken gently. When an eggshell cracks the egg is taken out of the sieve, and this goes on until only one unbroken egg is left. The ceremony is performed in each classroom, and the winning owner in the class gets a small money prize. At Stoke St. Gregory the cracked eggs are sent to the local Hospital; at Shepton Beauchamp their owners take them home for use in making pancakes.

March 1st   Lanark,
Whuppity Scoorie   Lanarkshire, Scotland

The curious name of Lanark's festival is equalled by the mystery of its origin, though, as in so many cases, it seems to be the survival of a pagan festival during which it was necessary to make a great deal of noise to scare away evil spirits and to protect the crops from damage.

On March 1st the bell in the steeple of the old parish church is tolled at 6 p.m., after a silence lasting four months. The children of Lanark have already gathered at the Lanark Cross, each equipped with a paper ball tied to a piece of string. The Provost, magistrates and town councillors are also there to watch the proceedings. At the first peal of the bell, which is one of the oldest in Europe, the children walk round the church three times, swinging their paper balls, after which they begin to hit each other with them in a mock battle. The excitement increases when pennies are thrown and the children scramble for them.

| March 25th | Tichborne and Cheriton, |
| *The Tichborne Dole* | Alresford, Hampshire |

Every year a huge bin containing thirty hundredweights of flour is placed on the steps of Tichborne House and, after a service conducted in Latin, the flour is distributed between the 900 people of Tichborne and the nearby hamlet of Cheriton. Men receive a gallon of flour, and women and children half a gallon. The ceremony is supervised by the head of the Tichborne family and his heir.

This ceremony, which began in the twelfth century, has a most interesting history. Lady Mabella Tichborne, wife of Sir Roger Tichborne, was on her death-bed and, wishing to help the needy of the parish, asked her husband to give land to the villagers, the produce of which would provide bread to be distributed every March 25th, which is Annunciation Day.

Sir Roger, who was either less generous by nature than his wife, or who had a warped sense of humour, took a faggot from the fire and declared that he would give as much land as she could encircle while the faggot was still burning. Lady Mabella, accepting the challenge, was carried out of the house, and by a superhuman effort succeeded in crawling round twenty-three and a half acres on her hands and knees.

This land is still called 'The Crawls', and still produces the thirty hundredweights of flour every year.

Before she died, Lady Mabella indulged in her own whimsy. She prophesied that if the custom were not kept up a generation of seven sons would be followed by another of seven daughters, after which the Tichborne family would die out. Then, presumably, she died happy.

The Dole was distributed regularly until 1799, when Sir Henry Tichborne, alarmed at the rowdiness that attended the ceremony, discontinued it. Coincidence or fate then decreed that Sir Henry's wife bore him seven sons, and when his eldest son inherited the estate, his wife had seven daughters, and the name of the owner of the estate changed. The Dole was resumed early in the nineteenth century.

Third Thursday in March   South Dalton,
Kipling Cotes Derby   Yorkshire

The Kipling Cotes Derby is the oldest horse flat race in the country, and has been run on the third Thursday in March for 450 years. It starts around noon and the course, which is four miles long, passes through five parishes, reputedly over the site of a Roman road.

The starting-point is in South Dalton and the finishing post is near Kipling Cotes Farm in the parish of Middleton. The rules for contestants are strict. Each rider must weigh at least ten stones; anybody under that weight who has stuffed his pockets with pieces of heavy metal is disqualified if this is discovered when weighing-in takes place on a coal merchant's scales.

Entrants pay £4, and the total stake money goes, not to the winner of the race, but to the rider who finishes second. This anomaly is explained by the fact that the winner receives the interest on the stock provided in 1618 by landowners of the district to endow the race for all time, and this amounts to between £5 and £6. The honour of winning, however, is more important than the amount of the prize money.

There was once an occasion when there were no entrants for the race. Rather than abandon it and break the tradition, officials walked a cart-horse over the course.

April 1st
All Fools' Day

> *The first April, some do say,*
> *Is set apart for All Fools' Day;*

> *But why the people call it so,*
> *Nor I, nor they themselves do know.*

The custom of involving a victim in a harmless practical joke on April 1st has been, and still is, practised with local variations in many countries, chiefly by children. Although the origin is obscure, there have been several interesting suggestions as to why April 1st is All Fools' Day. The most likely is that April 1st was the last day of the eight-day festivities which marked the New Year when it began on March 25th. This reason was put forward by a writer in the *Gentleman's Magazine* in 1766. He ended his letter by saying: 'It became a day of extraordinary mirth and festivity, especially among the lower sort, who are apt to pervert and to make bad use of institutions, which at first might be very laudable in themselves.'

A later writer in the same magazine suggests that 'the custom of imposing upon and ridiculing people on the first of April may have been an allusion to the mockery of the Saviour of the world by the Jews', and goes on to equate the practice with the Innocents' Day custom of imitating Herod's search for the child Jesus.

Another suggestion, in the *Public Advertiser* in 1789, lays the blame on Noah for sending a dove out of the ark before the waters had abated on the first day of the month. 'Anybody who was liable to forget the incident was punished by being sent on a fruitless errand similar to that ineffectual message upon which the bird was sent by the patriarch.'

There are traditional variations in nomenclature in different parts of the country just as there are different local jokes, but one constant factor is that the victim must be made an April Fool before midday. Failure to observe this rule is met with the justified rebuke that:

> *April Fools' Day's past and gone—*
> *You're the fool for thinking on.*

In the north of England an April Fool is a gowk, or cuckoo, as he is in Scotland too, where the day is also called Huntigowk Day. In Cheshire, variations on the word 'gawby' are used. Again, mainly in the north, April Fool becomes April Noddy.

Some traditional April Fools' Day jokes include sending someone to buy 'elbow grease', a book called *The Life of Adam's Father*, or 'a left-handed screwdriver'.

In 1860 a very elaborate hoax was perpetrated on several hundred important people in London, when they received an invitation to watch the ceremony of Washing the White Lions at the Tower of London. Admission, said the invitation card, would be by the White Gate. On April 1st crowds of people made their way to Tower Hill, only to find that there was neither a White Gate nor any white lions. One hopes that the practical joker, faced with a huge bill for printing and postage, thought that the discomfiture of his victims was worth the expense.

Easter

Though Easter is one of the three great Christian festivals, the name itself is pagan. According to the Venerable Bede, it comes from Eastre, or Eostre, the Anglo-Saxon goddess of Spring, and it is likely that when the Anglo-Saxons were converted to Christianity the old heathen festival became attached to the new Christian one. April was once called 'eosturmonath'. Another theory, however, suggests that the name comes from 'oster', meaning 'to rise'.

In the fourth century it was decided that the date of Easter should be the Sunday following the first full moon after the Vernal Equinox, March 21st. If the first moon is full on a Sunday, Easter Day is held on the next Sunday. Thus, Easter must fall between March 22nd and April 25th.

As the egg is a symbol of resurrection and new life, and has been since long before the Christian era, it is natural for eggs to be prominent at this season. They were forbidden food during Lent, but came into their own again on Easter Day and were given as presents to friends and servants.

Colouring eggs at Easter is a custom as old as the festival itself, and has a pagan origin that Christianity adapted for its own use. Easter eggs made of chocolate are a late development of the pace (paschal) egg which was hard-boiled with a dyed shell. Pace-egging, egg-rolling and the Pace-egging play are customs which can still be found in a few parts of the country.

Hares have always been associated with Easter, too, for the animal was sacred to Eostre. (The 'Easter bunny' is a modern mis-nomer.) Ritual hare-hunts once took place in England so that the goddess could be propitiated by a sacrifice.

Easter Monday has always been a day for sports and enjoyment, and in England and Wales is a Bank Holiday. Up to the end of the nineteenth century a favourite Easter Monday occupation was Lifting, or Heaving. Village lads decorated a chair with leaves and flowers and took it round to every house. The women of the house took turns to sit in the chair and were lifted up three times. For this the lads were rewarded with money and a kiss.

On Tuesday of Easter week the procedure was reversed. The girls took the chair round and lifted the men. This curious custom was supposed to commemorate Jesus rising from the dead, though probably it was a relic of a much older rite connected with encouraging the crops to grow tall.

In the larger towns Lifting became an excuse for hooliganism. Gangs of youths would seize any woman they met in the streets and hoist her up unceremoniously in spite of her protests. The following day women would do the same to unwilling men they chanced to meet, and often the chair was left at home. The distaste that respectable people felt for these proceedings helped to bring the custom to an end, though in country places it continued to be observed with proper decorum.

Palm Sunday	Hentland, Sellack and King's Capel,
Pax Cakes Distribution	near Ross-on-Wye, Herefordshire

Under the terms of the sixteenth-century will of Lady Scudamore, cakes and ale were presented to the congregation at the Palm Sunday service, and were consumed in the church. Lady Scudamore's aim was to promote peace and good fellowship in the parish before Easter started. A huge cake was made, the vicar cut the first slice for himself and the rest was passed round.

The large cake, and the ale too, have disappeared. Nowadays the cakes are small ones, bearing an impression of the Paschal Lamb. After the service the vicar gives one to each member of the congregation, saying as he does so, 'God and good neighbourhood!'

Maundy Thursday   Westminster Abbey,
Royal Maundy   London

Royal Maundy was begun in the reign of Edward III and is Britain's oldest charity. Until 1689 the sovereign went to Westminster Abbey every Maundy Thursday, the day before Good Friday, to wash the feet of the poor in memory of the service that Jesus performed for his disciples. Originally the recipients' feet were first washed in warm water scented with

sweet herbs by the Yeomen of the Laundry before the monarch washed them ceremoniously and kissed them. Since James II's time, however, the practice has been discontinued; in its place there is a distribution of specially minted money. The recipients are chosen from London parishes, and they are presented with silver penny, twopenny, threepenny and fourpenny coins to the value of a penny for each year of the sovereign's age.

A Yeoman of the Guard carries a golden tray on which are small leather purses, some white, some red, with long strings attached. The white purses contain the Maundy money; in the red ones is money given in place of the food and clothing formerly distributed. The queen, if she is present, and those taking part in the ceremony each carry a posy of flowers and sweet herbs (a traditional protection against the plague), and the clergy have linen towels on their shoulders as a reminder of the time when the feet-washing did take place.

In 1953, when Westminster Abbey was being prepared for the Coronation, the presentation of Maundy money took place in St. Paul's Cathedral, and since then the ceremony has been held in other cathedrals.

Maundy Thursday is the day of mandate (the Latin *mandatum* means 'command') and it refers to the words of Jesus after he had washed his disciples' feet: 'A new commandment I give unto you, that ye love one another.'

Good Friday   Tinsley Green,
Marbles Championship   near Crawley, Sussex

Marbles, a game known to the Romans, has been popular in Tinsley Green, and in many other places in Sussex and Surrey, since about 1600, when two rivals for the hand of a beautiful village girl fought a marbles battle.

The present Marbles Championship, the winner of which receives a silver cup, is played under the rules of the British Marbles Control Board. A concrete ring, six feet in diameter, is covered with sand. Each competitor of a team of six tries to knock out of the ring as many of the forty-nine marbles as possible with his glass 'tolley', which he grips between forefinger and thumb, and shoots without moving his whole hand.

After the contest the winner plays the previous year's champion in a match for which only thirteen marbles are placed in the ring.

Good Friday   Dunstable Downs,
Orange-rolling   Bedfordshire

This custom is connected with the better-known northern one of pace-egging and is the only one of its kind in southern England. Hundreds of children gather on Dunstable Downs and roll oranges down Pascombe Pit. This is said to be symbolic of the stone being rolled away from Jesus's tomb.

Good Friday   Midgley,
Pace-egg Play   Sowerby Bridge, Yorkshire

Most mummers' plays are performed at Christmas or on All Souls' Day, but at Midgley the play is associated with Easter, and is a variation of the usual play. It has similar characters, with an additional comic character called Tosspot. St. George is the hero and he battles against Bold Slasher, Bold Hector and the Black Prince of Paradine. Other members of the cast include the Fool, the Doctor and the King of Egypt. The Bugler sounds his bugle every time St. George makes an entrance.

The actors are boys from Calder High School. Their costumes are tunics, brightly coloured and covered with rosettes. They also wear large helmet-like hats bearing decorations and bells. The Doctor wears a top hat, and Tosspot has a straw tail to show his connection with the Devil. He also carries a basket in which at one time the spectators would put eggs, but nowadays money is presented to express appreciation of the play.

The Pace-egg Play can also be seen at Mytholmroyd, Hebden Bridge, Heptonstall, Luddenden and Todmorden.

Good Friday	St. Bartholomew the Great,
Poor Widows' Charity	Smithfield, London

After morning service on Good Friday, twenty-one poor widows over the age of sixty each receive sixpence, under the terms of a seventeenth-century bequest. The coins are placed on a tombstone in the churchyard, together with twenty-one hot cross buns. Each widow kneels by the stone, picks up her sixpence, walks over the stone, and is then given a bun and a further sum of money.

Easter Saturday	Bacup,
Nutters Dance	Lancashire

The Nutters Dance is an unusual form of the Morris dance, and is performed by the Britannia Coconut Dancers from one side of the town to the other, a distance of seven miles. The eight members of the team wear red and white skirts over black breeches, black clogs, white stockings and plumed white caps, and they perform with blackened faces.

They carry wooden discs, called 'nuts', made from the tops of bobbins, and they clap them as they dance against similar discs attached to their knees in a very complicated rhythm. The 'whipper-in' goes in front of the dancers to drive away evil spirits. Music used to be provided by a concertina player but is now performed by a band.

Easter Monday   Biddenden,
Biddenden Dole   Kent

Mary and Eliza Chulkhurst were Siamese twins, supposedly
born in 1100, though it is more likely to have been in 1500.
They died, almost at the same time, at the age of thirty-four,
and in their will they left twenty acres of land to provide bread
and cheese for the poor of the parish. Six acres of the 'Bread
and Cheese Land' were sold some years ago to the Rural
District Council for the building of houses, and the interest
on the proceeds of the sale has increased the income of the
charity.

At 10 a.m. on Easter Monday, two four-pound loaves and a
pound of cheese are given to those in need from the window of
one of the old workhouse cottages that were built on land once
belonging to Mary and Eliza. Also given away, to anybody who
wants one, are Biddenden cakes, which are really hard biscuits
bearing the impress of the joined sisters and the date 1100. The
Chulkhurst Charity also includes money gifts and nursing
treatment for the needy.

Easter Monday   Hallaton,
Bottle-kicking and Hare Pie-scrambling   Leicestershire

At a time, and by a person, unknown, a piece of land in
Hallaton was left to the rector in order to provide two hare pies,
two dozen loaves and a quantity of ale, all of which had to be
scrambled for on Easter Monday at a place called Hare Pie
Bank, a quarter of a mile south of the village. Hare is out of
season at this time of the year, so the pies are made of mutton,
veal or steak.

In the morning there is a service in the parish church, at
which the pies are blessed. After this they are cut up and
scrambled for. In the afternoon everybody gathers outside the
Fox Inn, and a brass band leads both contestants and spectators
to Hare Pie Bank.

There the bottle-kicking takes place. The bottles are in fact
small wooden casks, two of them filled with beer, the third
empty. Two teams are engaged in the contest, one from
Hallaton, the other from the neighbouring village of Medbourne.

The Bottle Keeper throws the first bottle, a filled one, into the air and lets it drop three times. This is a signal for the game to begin.

Any number of players can take part, and their object is to kick or handle the bottle over their own boundary. The boundaries are two streams, nearly a mile apart. The winning team keeps the beer, naturally. The second cask to be thrown up is the empty one. After the third cask has been fought for, its contents are shared among all the players at a ceremony at the market cross. The leader of the side which has claimed most of the three goals takes the first drink.

The hare pie scramble may go back to Saxon times as part of the Easter hare rites, in spite of the story of the bequest, but the bottle-throwing could well be older still, a survival of a pagan spring festival in which there was a symbolic struggle between winter and spring.

Easter Monday   Preston,
Pace-egging   Lancashire

Preston children roll hard-boiled brightly-coloured eggs down the slopes of Avenham Park in the afternoon. The custom may stem from a commemoration of the stone which was rolled away from Jesus's tomb, or it may be a reminder of the resurrection, the egg being a symbol of rebirth.

Egg-rolling is also an Easter attraction at Scarborough and Barton-upon-Humber.

Hocktide

Hocktide covers the Monday and Tuesday after Low Sunday, which is the Sunday after Easter. It was once a time for sports and games, and for the collection of money for the church and parish. The meaning of the name is uncertain, as is the origin of the festival. In some parts of the country, land rents were paid at Hocktide as well as at Michaelmas.

Men and women took turns to collect money for the needs of the church. Usually the men collected on Monday and the women on Tuesday, though in some places the order was reversed. From old records it seems that women were the better collectors. The favourite method was to stretch a rope across the road and impose a small toll on passers-by. The penalty for refusing to pay was to be bound with the rope and held prisoner until the collectors relented.

After the Reformation, Hocktide customs declined and had died out before the end of the seventeenth century. Only in one place, Hungerford, Berkshire, is there now any strong memory of the former jolly celebrations.

Second Tuesday after Easter   Hungerford,
Hocktide Tutti-men   Berkshire

Hungerford has no Mayor; the senior citizen of the town is the Constable, and he is elected on the second Tuesday after Easter at a special Hocktide Court, as are also the Portreeve, Bailiff and the Court of Feoffes.

Hungerford's great day begins about 9 a.m. with the Town Crier blowing his horn from the balcony of the Corn Exchange. The horn is a seventeenth-century copy of a fourteenth-century horn which was presented to the people of Hungerford by John of Gaunt as a token of the granting of certain manorial rights. In response to the sound the Bellman, or Assistant Bailiff, appears. He wears a scarlet and grey uniform with brass buttons, and his tall hat has a gold band round it. He rings his bell and commands the commoners (those who hold certain local rights in common lands) to attend the Court House. A refusal to obey incurs a fine of one penny.

The court meets in the Town Hall and elects the Constable and other officers, and two Tutti-men. Each Tutti-man carries a tall pole with a bunch of spring flowers (a *tutti*) tied to it with ribbons. There is an orange on the top.

The Tutti-men go out into the streets, accompanied by an Orange Scrambler carrying a sack full of oranges. He wears a tall hat with the tail feathers of a cock pheasant sticking out of it.

There are about a hundred commoners in Hungerford, and the Tutti-men visit all their houses, their aim being to get a penny from the men and a kiss from the women of the household, in exchange for an orange. Any oranges that are left after the women have been dealt with are scrambled for by the children who follow the Tutti-men. Pennies are also thrown for them.

The new Constable presides over a lunch held at the *Three Swans Hotel*. A special punch is drunk, the recipe of which is a secret. After lunch the ceremony of Shoeing the Colt takes place. A blacksmith pretends to drive nails into the shoes of new commoners and visitors—the 'colts'—and only stops when the victim cries 'Punch!' and hands over a contribution for another round of punch. More pennies and oranges are thrown from the windows for children to scramble over before the Tutti-men set off on their rounds again. They continue to collect tithes and kisses, and to give away oranges until the festival comes to an end in the evening. By that time the Tutti-men, who have by custom received 'hospitality' in each house might well have to be carried home!

London Customs

Thy famous Maire by pryncely governaunce,
With sword of justice thee ruleth prudently.
No Lord of Parys, Venyce or Floraunce
In dignitye or honour goeth to hym nigh.
He is exempler, loode-star and guye;
Principall patrone and rose orygynalle,
Above all Maires as maister most worthy:
London, thou art the flour of Cities all.

Few cities have a past as romantic and eventful as London's, and Londoners are both conscious of it and determined to maintain their ancient customs, however irrelevant they may seem in the twentieth century. Many of these customs are connected with the City's Livery Companies and date back to the fifteenth century and earlier. This unbroken link with medieval times is responsible for the splendid and colourful pageantry which is an essential part of the proceedings.

During the year Londoners and visitors to London have the opportunity of seeing, or participating in, many occasions that have their roots in London's history, among them the spectacular display of military pageantry known as Trooping the Colour, the Changing of the Guard, the Lord Mayor's Show, the Ceremony of the Keys at the Tower of London, Swan Upping, and the State Opening of Parliament. Other important ceremonies, though equally picturesque, are more private, and are attended only by members of the Livery Companies or by eminent men and women.

However, London has always something to offer to the ordinary person—sporting events, royal processions, military displays, art exhibitions, fairs, parades, and entertainments of all kinds from Cruft's Dog Show to the Boat Race, from badminton championships to veteran car rallies. Reference to newspapers and magazines such as *What's On In London* will provide the necessary information.

The following account of some of London's ceremonial observances is restricted to those which accent traditional aspects of London life, some well-known, others less so, but just as important in their quiet way.

January 5th (Twelfth Day Eve)	Theatre Royal,
Cutting the Baddeley Cake	Drury Lane

Twelfth Night used to be celebrated by a number of cere-monies, one of which was the cutting of the Twelfth Night Cake.

Robert Baddeley, a pastrycook who worked for the actor Samuel Foote, and who became an actor himself, died in 1794. In his will he left £100 to be invested, and directed that the interest should be used to purchase a Twelfth Night Cake with wine and punch for the members of the company playing at Drury Lane Theatre at the time. It was to be cut and eaten in the Green Room after the evening performance. By doing this, Baddeley ensured that he would never be forgotten in the theatre in which he played his first part.

The Baddeley Cake is now ceremoniously carried into the Green Room by two attendants dressed in eighteenth-century livery.

January 6th	Chapel Royal,
Royal Epiphany Gifts	St. James's Palace

Epiphany commemorates the visit of the Wise Men to the infant Jesus and the presentation of their gifts of gold, frankin-cense and myrrh. For 700 years it has been the custom of the reigning sovereign to make the same offerings at a choral

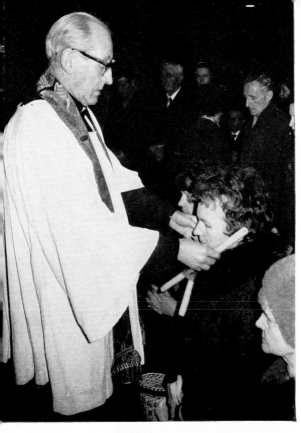

(*left*) The Blessing of the Throats ceremony at St. Etheldreda's Church in Ely Place, London

Plate 21

(*below*) Vintners' Procession to St. James's Garlick-hythe, London

Trooping the Colour, Horse Guards Parade, Whitehall, London

Plate 22

Swan Upping on the Thames between London and Henley

The Lord Mayor's Coach in the Lord Mayor's Show, in the City of London

Doggett's Coat and Badge Race from London Bridge to Chelsea

Plate 23

The Queen at the Royal Maundy Ceremony at Westminster Abbey, London

Plate 24

(*left*) Receiving Maundy Money at the Abbey ceremony

Celebration at the Chapel Royal. Two Gentlemen Ushers of the Royal Household present the royal gifts at the point in the service where the offertory is taken. The offering of gold is later exchanged for £1 notes, which are distributed to old age pensioners.

January 30th
Charles I Commemoration   Whitehall

King Charles I was executed on January 30th, 1649, and on the anniversary of his death adherents to the House of Stuart lay wreaths at the foot of his statue in Trafalgar Square, facing Whitehall. A procession of members of the Society of King Charles the Martyr and the Royal Stuart Society, led by choristers from the Church of St. Martin-in-the-Fields, goes from the church to the square, and a service is held there.

After King Charles's execution, the statue was ordered to be broken up for scrap, but the order was ignored and it was hidden in the vaults of St. Paul's Church, Covent Garden. In 1660, when the monarchy was revived, the statue was brought to light and erected in Trafalgar Square.

The present ceremony dates from 1892, and only on one occasion, on the death of Queen Victoria in 1901, has it not been observed.

February 3rd (St. Blaise's Day)   St. Etheldreda's Church,
Blessing of the Throats   Ely Place, Holborn

St. Blaise, a Bishop of Dalmatia in the third century, is the patron saint of throats, woolcombers and wild animals. He gained the first honour, while he was on his way to a martyr's death, by touching the throat of a boy who had a fishbone lodged in it, thus saving the boy's life. Woolcombers revere him because he was tortured with sharp iron combs, such as are used in carding wool.

To commemorate the miracle that the saint wrought, a service is held every year at St. Etheldreda's Church. Two candles, tied together to form a St. Andrew's Cross, are blessed by the priest. Sufferers from throat afflictions kneel before the altar and the priest holds the lighted candles under their chins and touches their throats with the ribbon that ties the candles together. He intones a short prayer, and St. Blaise does the rest.

Ely Place is a *cul-de-sac*, and the one place in London where the watch is still kept and the police do not go. Every night a liveried Beadle calls 'Ten o'clock and all's well', just when the bugler is sounding his call at the Tower of London. As late as Queen Victoria's reign the Queen's writ was not valid there and the inhabitants were free from taxation. Ely Place is still controlled by commissioners elected by the householders, and until recently they were responsible for paving, lighting and watering.

February 20th (on or near)   St. Botolph's Church,
Sir John Cass Commemoration Service   Aldgate

Sir John Cass, a wealthy Alderman of the City of London, was born on February 20th, 1661, and died in 1718. He was interested in the education of children, and in his will he provided for the building and upkeep of a school in Aldgate. St. Botolph's Church now stands on the site of the school. It is said that while signing his will he suffered a haemorrhage of the lungs and that his quill pen became stained with his blood.

A commemoration service is held on or near the anniversary of his birth at St. Botolph's. It is attended by the staff, pupils and governors of the Sir John Cass College and the Sir John Cass Foundation School. On that day the girls of the school wear a red quill in their berets as a reminder of the bloodstained quill used by their benefactor.

Ash Wednesday
Cakes and Ale Sermon   St. Paul's Cathedral

John Norton, a member of the Worshipful Company of Stationers in the reign of James I, left money in his will to provide that his fellow members should gather in Stationers' Hall and then attend a service in St. Faith's Chapel in the crypt of old St. Paul's every Ash Wednesday. The sermon is preached by the Chaplain to the Stationers' Company.

A procession of members of the Stationers' Company, dressed in their traditional velvet caps and furred gowns, goes from Stationers' Hall to the Cathedral. It is headed by a Junior

Beadle; the Senior Beadle, the Wardens and the Master bring up the rear. Cakes and ale are waiting for the members after the service, when they return to the Hall.

April 5th (on or near)   Church of St. Andrew Undershaft,
John Stow's Quill Pen Ceremony   Leadenhall Street

John Stow (1525–1605) was a tailor who later became an antiquary. He was the author of *The Survey of London* (1598), a classic chronicle of the London of his day. On or near April 5th, the anniversary of his death, a service is held in St. Andrew Undershaft Church, where he was buried. It is attended by the Lord Mayor, two Sheriffs and other City and church dignitaries.

In the church there is an effigy of John Stow, made of marble and alabaster, which represents him writing his book, a quill pen in his hand. After the service the Lord Mayor replaces the old quill pen by a new one. The old one is given to the school of which the winner of the annual John Stow Essay Contest is a member.

Last Sunday in April
The Tyburn Walk   Marble Arch

During the religious persecutions of the sixteenth and seventeenth centuries a large number of people were executed on the Tyburn gallows, which stood on a spot near the present Marble Arch. The last execution took place in 1783.

Many of the victims were Catholics, and to commemorate their deaths, and those of others executed on Tower Hill, in St. Paul's Churchyard and in Lincoln's Inn Fields, a pilgrimage, usually headed by a prelate of the Roman Catholic Church, is made on the last Sunday in April.

The procession starts from the site of the old Newgate Prison (now the Central Criminal Court), follows the route along which the martyrs were dragged on hurdles, and finishes at the site of Tyburn gallows. Stops on the way are made at St. Etheldreda's Church in Ely Place, SS. Anselm and Cecilia's in Kingsway, St. Giles's in-the-Fields, and at St. Patrick's in Soho Square.

Benediction is given upon the site of Tyburn Convent (which was bombed during the Second World War) in Bayswater, near where the gallows stood.

The walk was started in the early years of this century, by one man and his sister, but nowadays it attracts a large number of pilgrims and spectators.

May 21st   Wakefield Tower,
Ceremony of the Lilies and the Roses   Tower of London

Henry VI was murdered in the Tower of London on May 21st, 1471. During his reign he founded Eton College and King's College, Cambridge. On the anniversary of his death a representative from both seats of learning, usually the Provost, joins a procession to the Wakefield Tower, and lilies and roses are placed on the white marble slab which marks the spot where the king was killed. The slab was put down in 1923, the year in which the annual ceremony began.

Eton provides the lilies, which are tied up with light blue silk, and King's College the red roses, which are tied with a purple ribbon. The simple service includes the reciting of a

Latin prayer which Henry VI composed.

Second Saturday in June   Horse Guards Parade,
Trooping the Colour   Whitehall

The military pageant known as Trooping the Colour was first held in 1755 as a tribute to George II, the last king to fight personally in battle. It became an annual event in 1805, to celebrate the birthday of George III, and is now held near June 13th, the Queen's official birthday.

Trooping the Colour is a survival of the old custom of using colours for identification and for rallying points in battle. This was necessary when the army included mercenaries of different nationalities whose knowledge of English was limited. 'Troop' means a combination of music and marching.

The Queen's Household Brigade takes part in a display of precision-marching, the climax of which is the ceremonial carrying of Colours along the assembled Parade. Each battalion of Foot Guards has a turn in providing an Escort for the Colour.

When the Queen arrives she inspects the Parade. Then comes the Trooping ceremony and the march past, at which she takes the salute. At the end of the marching the Queen rides to the head of the Guards contingents and leads them to Buckingham Palace, where she takes a last salute before they march away. The Escort to the Colour mounts guard at the Palace.

June 24th
Election of Sheriffs   Great Hall of the Guildhall

On Midsummer Day Liverymen of the Guilds—the freemen of the City Companies—meet at Common Hall, in the Great Hall of the Guildhall, to elect two Sheriffs and other high officers of the City of London, to serve for a year.

After the Lord Mayor and the City's officers have arrived and taken their places on a dais covered with sweet-smelling herbs, the mace and sword are placed on a table in front of them. The Common Crier calls for silence, bared heads, and the removal of all unauthorised persons ('on pain of imprisonment'). After the minutes of the previous Common Hall have been read, the Recorder of London announces that the election can begin.

The City Marshal and the Sword-bearer lead the Lord Mayor, those Aldermen who are former Sheriffs, the Recorder and the Town Clerk to the South Court as a sign that the election will be free and fair. The mace is left on the table on the dais to show that the Lord Mayor's authority must be observed even when he is absent from the Hall. In the South Court the sword of state is laid in a bed of roses (the rose being the emblem of silence).

After the Sheriffs, the Chamberlain, the Bridge Masters and Ale Conners have been elected, the Lord Mayor and the other officers return to the Great Hall to hear the results. Newly-elected Sheriffs are eligible for election as Lord Mayor.

June 24th
The Knollys Red Rose Rent The Mansion House

This ancient custom, revived in 1924, commemorates the fining of Sir Robert Knollys for his misdemeanour in building a footbridge without permission across Seething Lane to connect two houses he owned there. This took place when Sir Robert returned to London in 1346 after fighting in the French wars. The City Fathers decided that the offence was not a serious one, and the fine was a red rose, to be plucked from his garden in Seething Lane and presented to the Lord Mayor every Midsummer Day.

Sir Robert paid his annual tribute cheerfully until old age and illness prevented him from carrying on. Nowadays the duty is observed by the churchwardens of the Church of All Hallows by the Tower. They carry a red rose on an altar cushion up the stairs of the Mansion House and solemnly present it to the Lord Mayor.

Thursday after July 4th
Vintners' Procession Upper Thames Street

When the Worshipful Company of Vintners have elected their new Master and Wardens, usually on the Thursday after July 4th, they walk in procession from the Vintners' Hall in

Upper Thames Street to the Church of St. James, Garlickhythe, to attend a special service.

The procession, which starts about 5.30 p.m., is preceded by two wine porters in white smocks and top hats, whose job is to sweep the street with birch brooms so that the members of the Company 'slip not on any foulness'—something that was much more likely to happen 700 years ago when the decree was first made. As a further reminder of the state of the roads in medieval times, the Vintners carry posies of herbs and flowers, the scent of which counteracts 'noxious flavours and ill vapours'.

With the Vintners in this procession are the Company's Swan Markers and Barge Master—a reminder that, between them, the Vintners, the Dyers and the Queen own all the swans on the Thames between London Bridge and Henley.

Last Monday in July (on or about)   The River Thames,
Swan Upping   between London and Henley

Of the City Livery Companies, the Vintners' Company and the Dyers' Company alone have the right, which they share with the Queen, of keeping a 'game of swans' on the River Thames between London Bridge and Henley. The Queen's Swan Keeper, and the Swan Wardens and Swan Markers appointed by the two Companies, are responsible each year for the Swan Upping, which begins when the cygnets are about two months old.

The ceremony was instituted in the reign of Elizabeth I, when a Royal Licence was needed to own a swan. It is performed from skiffs, and the men in them round up the swans so that the ownership of the cygnets can be established. The gaily beflagged craft start at Southwark and sail up the Thames as far as Henley.

The convoy is commanded by the Queen's Swan Keeper wearing scarlet livery. Two skiffs fly the Queen's Standard, and they are followed by four more, two belonging to each of the City Companies. The Dyers' Company Swan Master wears blue livery, and the Vintners' green. The oarsmen have jerseys and conical woollen hats in red, white and blue stripes.

Swans belonging to the Vintners' Company have a nick on each side of the bill; those belonging to the Dyers are nicked on one side only. Unmarked swans belong to the Queen. It takes about a week to catch and mark all the swans, as about 600 birds have to be examined.

August 1st (as near as possible to)	London Bridge
Doggett's Coat and Badge Race	to Chelsea Bridge

This annual rowing race, the oldest competitive rowing event in the world, is held under the auspices of the Worshipful Company of Fishmongers, and is for six Thames Watermen. Thomas Doggett was an Irish actor who, in 1715, instituted the race in honour of the accession to the throne of George I. When he died he left money for the race to be continued, and the disposition of the legacy was entrusted to the Fishmongers' Company.

The champion oarsman receives a scarlet livery (it was originally orange) with silver buttons and a large silver badge on the left arm. The other competitors get a silver cup. Only watermen who have just completed their apprenticeship can take part; thus no one is allowed to enter the competition more than once. So many men wish to take part that heats have to be rowed off beforehand.

The race starts from the Old Swan Pier at London Bridge, and finishes at Cadogan Pier, Chelsea Bridge, where the *Old White Swan Inn* used to stand. The contestants have to row against the tide, and the race demands great strength and skill. A barge follows the rowers, and on it are some of the past winners wearing their coats and badges. The names of the Doggett's Coat and Badge Race winners are on record from 1791.

September 21st (or nearest convenient day)	Newgate to
Christ's Hospital Boys' March	the Mansion House

Every year on St. Matthew's Day three hundred Bluecoat boys from Horsham, and twenty-five girls from the Hertford school, led by their own band, walk through the City of London to St. Sepulchre's Church, Newgate. After the service, which is attended by the Lord Mayor, Sheriffs and Aldermen, they proceed to the Mansion House of the City of London to be entertained by the Lord Mayor. Each boy and girl also receives a newly-minted silver coin.

This ceremony is designed to keep strong an old link between Christ's Hospital, which was founded in Newgate Street in 1553, and the Mansion House. Early this century the boys' school moved to Horsham and the girls' to Hertford. The boys still wear their traditional Tudor uniform, slightly modified. It consists of a dark blue gown, leather belt, linen bands and yellow stockings.

September 29th
Election of the Lord Mayor Guildhall

Michaelmas Day has seen the annual election of the Lord Mayor of London since 1546, and he has been chosen by the votes of the City's eighty-one Livery Companies since 1715. This ceremony takes place in the Guildhall, where the platform on which the Lord Mayor sits is strewn with herbs, as it was in medieval times, as a protection against both plague and witchcraft.

The candidates are chosen from Aldermen who have served a term of office as Sheriff. On the day of the election a high wooden fence, containing a number of doors, is built in front of the Guildhall, and behind each door stands the Beadle of a Livery Company in uniform and three-cornered hat. His job is to see that no unauthorised person gets into the Guildhall during the ceremony.

After a service in the Church of St. Lawrence Jewry, the Lord Mayor, two Sheriffs and twenty-six Aldermen in their scarlet gowns go from the Mansion House to Guildhall, where they are each presented with a nosegay of flowers. They take their seats on the platform and the Common Crier, wigged and gowned and carrying the mace, orders silence. The Recorder of London explains the proceedings to the Liverymen; then the Lord Mayor and Aldermen who have been Lord Mayors withdraw with the Recorder, leaving the mace on the table.

The Common Serjeant reads out the names of the two Aldermen eligible to be candidates. The first name is usually greeted by the Liverymen with a shout of 'All!', and the second name by 'Next year!' If there are more names to be considered they are received with 'Later on!' or 'Another time!'

The two candidates are led to the Aldermen's Court, which consists of the thirteen Aldermen who make the final decision. The candidates are questioned in whispers, the Aldermen record their votes with the Town Clerk, and the Lord Mayor gives his casting vote if one is needed. The Recorder announces the result.

The Lord Mayor-elect, now wearing his chain of office, makes a speech. The Common Crier closes the proceedings, and the Lord Mayor and his successor-to-be leave the Hall to the sound of trumpets. They appear together in the porch, the City bells ring out, and then they drive in the state coach to the Mansion House, which has been the official residence of London's Lord Mayors since 1753.

First Sunday in October   St. Mary-at-Hill Church,
Fish Harvest Festival   Billingsgate

St. Mary-at-Hill, in Lovat Lane, is the parish church of Billingsgate, the fish market. At a service held on the first Sunday in October thirty-nine different varieties of fish are offered for blessing by men working in the fish trade. The number represents the thirty-nine Articles of the Anglican faith. The ante-chapel is decorated with fish and nets, and sometimes with a boat. Fruit and flowers are also displayed.

The service is usually attended by the Aldermen and members of the Common Council of the Ward.

Between Martinmas and Michaelmas
Horseshoes and Nails Rent Royal Courts of Justice, Strand

One of London's oldest customs is observed at a special court held at the Royal Courts of Justice at an agreed date between Martinmas and Michaelmas. It has been going on since the early thirteenth century at least.

The Annual Quit Rent Service is conducted by the Queen's Remembrancer. He opens the proceedings with a proclamation: 'Tenants and occupiers of a piece of waste ground called "The

Moors" in the County of Salop, come forth and do your service.'

The City Solicitor, who represents the Corporation (the tenants and occupiers of the said land), takes up a bill-hook and hatchet, and cuts up two small faggots, in discharge of the debt. He hands the pieces to the Remembrancer, who receives them with the comment, 'Good service'.

The Remembrancer's second proclamation is: 'Tenants and occupiers of a certain tenement called "The Forge" in the parish of St. Clement Danes, in the County of Middlesex, come forth and do your service.' (Australia House in the Strand now stands on the site of the forge.)

The City Solicitor, again representing the tenants and occupiers, counts out six large horseshoes and sixty-one nails, and the Remembrancer says, 'Good number'.

The horseshoes and nails, said to be hundreds of years old, are brought out each year specially for the ceremony. For the rest of the year they are kept at the City Solicitor's office in Guildhall.

November 8th
Installation of the Lord Mayor   Guildhall

The installation of London's Lord Mayor takes place on the eve of Lord Mayor's Day, six weeks after he is elected. The ceremony starts with a luncheon at the Mansion House, presided over by the Lord Mayor and the Lord Mayor-elect. The guests are the members of the retiring Lord Mayor's Livery Company and the Liverymen of the new Lord Mayor's Company. When the procession is ready to leave for Guildhall, the Lord Mayor-elect leaves by a side door to show that he is not yet in full possession of the mayoral rights. The Lord Mayor leaves in semi-state. He does not wear the SS collar and badge, but only the chain of his Shrievalty.

At Guildhall the Lord Mayor presides at the Court of Aldermen for the last time. When the procession reaches the Great Hall the Lord Mayor takes the chair, the Lord Mayor-elect sits on his left, and the Town Clerk calls upon the latter to sign a declaration. Then the Lord Mayor leaves his chair and sits in the one relinquished by his successor, to show that he is now no longer the principal actor.

The insignia of office are then transferred from the outgoing Lord Mayor to the incoming one, and this part of the ceremony is performed in complete silence. The new Lord Mayor receives the Crystal Sceptre, the Seal of Mayoralty, and the City Purse, which is believed to have been given to the City by Elizabeth I. The City Chamberlain first presents them to the old Lord Mayor, who presents them to the new one. The Sword-bearer ceremoniously delivers up the pearl sword, given to the City by Elizabeth I in 1571. The Common Crier presents the mace and, equipped with all the insignia of office, the new Lord Mayor is Mayor indeed.

After signing various documents the new Lord Mayor is given the keys of the City, the hospital seals and other symbols of high office. The ceremony ends with a fanfare of trumpets, and church bells peal as the two men return together to the Mansion House.

Second Saturday in November
Lord Mayor's Show   Mansion House, Guildhall, Law Courts
This is the day when the new Lord Mayor officially takes office. It is a great day of civic pageantry. The Lord Mayor's Show procession dates back at least to the reign of King John, and has always provided an opportunity for a display of the City's great wealth. The Livery Companies have always played a prominent part in the proceedings.

The mile-long procession of decorated floats is picturesque and interesting, but the Lord Mayor's coach, drawn by six horses each carrying a hundredweight of harness, which brings up the rear, is the highlight which draws the cheers and gasps of the crowd. The bewigged coachman and liveried attendants, and the coach with its gilded carvings, painted panels, shining plate glass, linings of crimson silk and gold, and scarlet wheels, are straight out of a fairy tale. The coach is over two hundred years old and weighs nearly four tons. It is extremely uncomfortable to ride in, as there are no springs, and the Lord Mayor must be glad that this is the only occasion on which he is required to use it.

He sits inside with the Sword-bearer and Mace-bearer, carrying their emblems of office, facing him. The footmen walk beside the coach, and scarlet-clad grooms are at the horses' heads. The City Marshal on horseback accompanies the Lord Mayor, and a guard of honour is provided by the Company of Pikemen and Musketeers, drawn from the Honourable Artillery Company.

The Lord Mayor, together with his Sheriffs and Aldermen, goes to Guildhall from the Mansion House, and there addresses of loyalty are presented to him. He then proceeds to the Royal Courts of Justice in the Strand and, standing before the Lord Chief Justice and the Judges, he promises to perform his duties faithfully.

In the evening a magnificent banquet is held at Guildhall. Nowadays the Prime Minister gives a major political speech, and the Archbishop of Canterbury proposes a toast to the hosts on behalf of the guests.

Fairs

FAIRS have formed one of the most important features of English life for hundreds of years; and although those which survive are but pale shadows of their former selves and are given over to pleasure rather than commerce, they still fulfil some of their original functions as places at which to meet friends, forget the cares of life and enjoy the entertainments provided.

Fairs were particularly important in the Middle Ages, when life was hard and boring, and the occasion for an annual holiday and a great trading event was eagerly seized upon. Their decline in the last two hundred years is due to the increase in the opportunities we have for pleasure and leisure, greater ease in travelling and the breakdown of small, self-sufficient communities.

Many fairs are much older than the charters which gave them official recognition, and reflect the Church's policy of turning pagan festivals into Christian feasts. The origin of some of them goes back to Roman times ('feria' is Latin for holiday), but when Christianity spread over Britain, fairs were related to the feast day of a saint, particularly the saint to which the parish church was dedicated. The first part of the day was spent at Mass; the rest was given up to dancing, games, and trading from booths and stalls that were often set up in or near the churchyard.

When trading became the important part of the proceedings, many towns and villages applied for a charter for their fair, to give it legal status. Some fairs received their charters in Norman times, others in medieval times. By the thirteenth century the golden age of fairs had begun; the best-known had been granted charters—nearly 5,000 were given between 1200 and 1400— some as a reward for services to the king, both on and off the field of battle.

Monasteries, colleges, great families and powerful land-owners received charters in order to collect revenue from the stallholders. Only a trading fair established by royal charter is entitled to be called a 'fair'; one which marks a church's patronal festival and is unchartered should be more properly called a 'wake' or a 'feast'.

During the Middle Ages the trade guilds were very power-ful, and guild laws were strictly enforced. Strangers to a town were allowed to embark on trade only while a fair was in pro-gress, when the normal trading restrictions were relaxed. An Act of 1331 decreed that every Lord of the Manor should pro-claim how long the fair should last, and there were penalties for anyone who continued to sell when the fair had officially finished. In Norman times ordinary courts were replaced by Courts of Pie Powder. The words are a corruption of *pieds poudreux*— 'dusty-footed'—and refer to the wandering pedlars who travel-led from fair to fair, coming even from France and other European countries, trying to earn an uncertain living. They would naturally arrive at a fairground very travel-stained and dusty, especially about the feet.

A Court of Pie Powder was set up to deal with disputes among the stallholders and to maintain order during the period of the fair. Offenders were punished on the spot, and might be fined or put in the stocks or pillory, there to receive the jeers of the onlookers and anything that might be thrown at them.

Pie Powder Courts were still operating in the nineteenth century, until the County Courts Act of 1888 gave the fair owners the chance to surrender their rights to the Crown. One of the few surviving examples of a Pie Powder Court is attached to Bristol's Tolzey Court. It is opened outside the *Stag and*

Hounds Inn in Old Market Street every September 30th at 10 a.m., even though St. James's Fair has not been held since 1838.

Merchants, pedlars and visitors to a fair knew that they could enter the town and begin to trade when they saw that a wooden glove or hand had been hung over the Guildhall window or outside the church, or had been paraded by the Town Crier. 'The glove is up!' was a signal that the fair had begun. The custom probably has its origin in Saxon times when a local judge gave permission for a fair to be held, and his decision had to be ratified by the king, who sent a glove to show his approval.

Until the Reformation the organisation of many fairs was in the hands of Church officials and they became an important source of revenue for the Church. Sometimes a fair was established around the shrine of a saint. When the annual occasion became disorderly and uncontrollable, as often happened, a reaction against fairs set in, and by the seventeenth century, denounced by the Puritans, they had begun to lose their popularity and their commercial importance, and this process was later speeded up by the changes that the following centuries brought.

The great season for fairs was the autumn, when the hard and exhausting work on the farms had been done and there was time for relaxation and merry-making before winter put an end to outdoor pursuits. Many of the autumn fairs had no charter. They were called Hiring or Mop Fairs, and were particularly important in the north of England. They began in the middle of the fourteenth century after the Black Death had caused a shortage of agricultural workers and servants. These were usually hired for a year, from Michaelmas to Michaelmas, so at the fair servants looked for new employers and employers looked for new servants. Men and women in search of employment wore a token of their craft or calling: a cowman or a milkmaid showed a tuft of cow hair, a shepherd put sheep's wool in his hat or carried a crook, a carter dangled a piece of whipcord or a whip, a groom displayed a sponge, and a maid carried a mop or wore a white apron. They paraded themselves before prospective masters and mistresses and, if they were lucky, were hired.

The contract was sealed when a 'hiring' penny was put into the worker's hand. By the nineteenth century the penny had become a shilling. The hiring penny was used to buy a piece of ribbon to replace the craft token.

In some places a Runaway Mop Fair was held a week or two after the Mop Fair. This was to give another opportunity to those who had not already found a situation, or to allow the contract to be set aside by both masters or servants who regretted their choice.

After the religious element of fairs had disappeared at the Reformation, trading became the important aspect. Each fair tended to specialise in one commodity and many became famous for their speciality. There were many horse fairs, and others given over to the sale of ponies, sheep, cows, geese, cheese and herrings among other things. Though the old name of the fair may linger on (such as Nottingham's Goose Fair) it is unlikely nowadays (though there are exceptions) that a single specimen of what the fair was once noted for will be on sale. No longer do we go to the fair to buy a year's supply of cloth or salt, to hire a servant or replenish our animal stock. We go to enjoy a ride on the roundabouts or the Dodgem cars, test our skill at shooting clay pipes on the move or spinning balls, patronise the fortune-teller, win a plastic bowl of goldfish at the Hoopla stall or a hideous vase at Bingo, and disorganise our digestive systems with candyfloss, peanuts and hot dogs.

Fairs, Past and Present

The great name among fairs was that of St. Bartholomew, which was held at Smithfield in London for over 700 years. It was the biggest of London's fairs, and certainly the most notorious. When it came to an end in 1855 respectable people breathed a sigh of relief.

St. Bartholomew's Fair received its charter in 1133, and almost from its beginning it attracted a great number of people of bad character: thieves, beggars, harlots and tricksters of every kind. The nastiest and most sordid side of human nature was on parade, and the occasion was an opportunity for the display of gluttony, lechery, licentiousness and dishonesty.

Very often the highlight was the public hanging of criminals.

At one time the fair was the chief cloth fair of the country, and cattle, pewter and leather were also sold in great quantities. There were always many exhibitions and sideshows; there were plays, performing animals, conjurers and jugglers, and quack doctors were much in evidence. Ben Jonson (c. 1573–1637) wrote a play called *Bartholomew Fair*, a long, sprawling affair which gives a vivid and horrific picture of what went on. Charles II extended the duration of the fair from three to fourteen days, but in 1708, because of riotous behaviour, the time was reduced to three days again.

In 1839 rents of the stalls and booths were doubled, and many of the showmen could not afford the increase. Some gave up altogether, while others transferred their exhibitions to Islington. Up to 1850 the Lord Mayor kept up the tradition of reading the proclamation that opened the fair. Five years later the fair was abolished as a nuisance, and it came to an end, regretted by few.

The greatest of the English provincial fairs was held at Sturbridge, near Cambridge. King John granted its charter in 1211, though the fair was in existence long before his time. It was held on St. Bartholomew's Day and for three weeks afterwards. The booths were erected on the open fields in rows, so as to form streets; the main one was nearly half a mile long, and the fairground became almost like a small town. There were booths for eating and drinking, taverns and coffee-houses. Great quantities of cloth were sold, as well as hops, hosiery, brassware and knives. Merchants came from the Baltic countries with furs and amber, from Flanders with linen and from Genoa with velvets and silks. Tin from Cornwall was on sale, iron from Sussex, salt from Worcestershire, and lead from Derbyshire. Students from the University bought their books at the fair.

During the reign of Queen Elizabeth I, the City and the University quarrelled over the fees paid by the stallholders, and in 1589 the queen settled the dispute by giving the City a charter to control the booths, and the University the right to supervise weights and measures and to control the sale of bread, wine and ale.

Sturbridge Fair was held for the last time in 1855, though the proclamation of the opening went on until 1933, with fewer and fewer people attending the 'non-event'.

St. Ives, in Huntingdonshire, has a fair that dates from a charter granted by Henry I in 1100. The fair is actually older than the town, and the town owes its existence to the fair. A fair dedicated to St. Ive was once held at Slepe during Easter week, and the houses from which trading was carried on and round which booths were erected became the nucleus of the town of St. Ives.

The fair lasted for eight days rather than the customary three, and in the thirteenth century it was one of the most important fairs in the country, noted particularly for textiles and hides. During the Hundred Years' War it declined in usefulness and importance. Now it exists only as a pleasure fair held for one day in October, though there is also a special market held on Whit Monday.

The last of the once great fairs of England was the Bishop's Fair of Winchester in Hampshire, which had the earliest charter of them all. Its duration of three days was extended by Henry I, again by Stephen, and under Edward II it became twenty-four days. Eventually it settled down with sixteen.

It was held on a hill-top site near the Long Barrow, which indicates that its origins reach far back into antiquity. Wool, tin, spices and wine were its specialities. The Bishop of Winchester had complete authority over the fair, and while it was on the Mayor and Bailiffs of the city were dismissed. The Court of Pavilions, which possessed even wider powers than the Court of Pie Powder, was the only court allowed to sit for the sixteen days. Not only did it deal with cases arising from occurrences at the fair, but it dealt with all the city's affairs.

For seven leagues around the city no trading was allowed. Everything that was bought and sold had to be bought and sold at the fair. The Bishop's staff inspected all food and drink, and were empowered to fine stallholders whose goods were not of the required standard. The town's shopkeepers closed their shops for the duration of the fair. It was not worth their while keeping them open for their prices were undercut by traders at the fair. Even innkeepers found the period unprofitable; visitors to the fair could get all they wanted on the spot.

Eventually the Bishop of Winchester grew too ambitious. He tried to force Southampton to become part of Winchester Fair, which meant that Southampton shopkeepers had to close too, and everything, except food, was taken to Winchester. All bridges, roads and tracks into Winchester were watched to make sure that nobody entered the city without paying a toll.

Resentment against the Bishop and the restrictions he imposed on normal trading grew strong every time the fair was held, and when it was over the citizens welcomed the return of the Mayor and the resumption of their ordinary way of life.

Owing to wars in the fourteenth century overseas merchants were not able to visit the fair and it lost much of its importance. The Bishop's power was greatly reduced when Winchester was granted the right to hold two fairs over which he had no control, and the Bishop's Fair came to an end, to the relief of the citizens of Winchester and to the joy of the shopkeepers.

Calendar of Fairs

FEBRUARY

King's Lynn, Norfolk

King's Lynn Fair has been held on February 14th, Valentine's Day, since the early eleventh century. Only the Plague in 1666 and two World Wars prevented its appearance. It lasts for six days, and is one of the earliest fairs of the year. It has a ceremonial opening by the Mayor who, with his party, has the privilege of being first to ride on the roundabouts.

April

Lincoln, Lincolnshire

Lincoln Fair lasts for a whole week at the end of April. Its charter was granted by Charles II.

Devizes, Wiltshire

Devizes has two Statute Fairs, one in April, the other in October. Neither has fixed dates.

May

St. Mark's Fair, Abingdon, Berkshire

In medieval times Abingdon had three fairs: St. Mark's, St. Edmund's, and the Michaelmas Hiring Fair. The Election of the Mayor of Ock Street (q.v.), held on the Saturday nearest to June 20th, is the only part of St. Edmund's Fair which has survived. St. Mark's Fair is held early in May, and the Hiring Fair on the Monday and Tuesday before October 11th. The Runaway Fair is held the following Monday.

Stow-on-the-Wold, Gloucestershire

Stow Fair was granted a charter in 1476, by Edward IV. It began as a sheep fair, but with the decline of the Cotswold wool trade it changed over to horses. The Horse Fair is still held on May 12th, with harness and farm equipment on sale, and there is another fair on October 24th.

St. Ethelbert's Fair, Hereford, Herefordshire

Henry I granted the town its charter, and in its early days the fair began on May 19th and lasted for nine days. The Bishop's bailiff was charged with calling together all the Bishop's tenants so that they could attend on him as he proclaimed the fair open from High Cross. Then the bailiff became the chief magistrate. He held court at the Bishop's Palace and there received the stallholders' tolls. This system was not popular as it led to abuses, and the citizens of Hereford became at loggerheads with their Bishop.

When fairs declined in importance, the nine days was reduced to two. By 1840, the rights of the Court of Pie Powder were transferred to the Corporation of Hereford, and the Bishop's profits decreased dramatically—to twelve and a half bushels of the best wheat.

St. Ethelbert's Fair, now held on the first Wednesday after May 2nd, is a pleasure fair only, though the custom of the Mayor handing over the Bishop's wheat at the opening ceremony has been revived.

JUNE

New Fair, Appleby, Westmorland

This used to be a great meeting-place for gipsies, and hundreds of caravans made their way to Appleby during June and lined the roads into the town. The fair is still devoted to horses, but the sale of sheep and cattle has died out.

Bradford, Yorkshire

Two fairs are held in June: the Annual Fair, beginning on June 8th and lasting for three days, and another beginning on June 29th, also for three days.

JULY

Lammas Fair, Exeter, Devon

Lammas Fair was once held on July 31st and for the following two days, but it now opens on the Tuesday before the third Wednesday in July and continues until the Friday. The medieval custom of displaying a glove to open the fair was revived in 1939 after a lapse of many years. The glove is carried on a blue and white pole, and the fair is proclaimed open at the Cattle Market, Exe Island, Fore Street, and at the site of the East Gate. Roads from all parts of Devon, central and eastern England meet at Exeter, and Lammas Fair was one of the most important trade fairs in the south-west.

Honiton Fair, Honiton, Devon

The fair dates from 1257 and used to be held during the first three days in Whit week. Now it takes place on the Tuesday and Wednesday after July 19th. It is officially opened by the Town Crier, who carries a gilt glove on a decorated staff. 'Oyez! Oyez! Oyez!' he calls. 'The glove is up and the fair has begun! No man shall be arrested until the glove is taken down! God save the Queen!'

The glove is set up over the door of an inn, and children scramble for hot pennies thrown from the inn's windows.

Cattle and moorland ponies can still be bought at the fair, though it is now chiefly a pleasure fair.

Horn Fair, Ebernoe, near Petworth, Sussex

On July 25th (St. James's Day) a horned sheep is roasted in a pit. The head projects over the edge of the pit so that it remains uncooked. Then the head is cut off, and the roast mutton from the animal's body is eaten by the players of an annual cricket match. The batsman with the highest score is presented with the sheep's horns.

Lamb Fair, Findon, Sussex

Lamb Fair is held on July 14th, and anything up to 2,500 lambs may be sold on that day. At the Great Fair, on September 14th, more than 10,000 sheep are sold.

AUGUST

Cranham, Gloucestershire

On the second Monday in August a deer is roasted, and eaten at a lunch given to local people and invited guests. At the fair, a tug-of-war contest is held between teams from Cranham and Upton St. Leonards.

Horse Fair, Brigg, Lincolnshire

Brigg Fair has been held since the thirteenth century, and is an occasion when gipsies converge on the town on August 5th. They gallop their horses through the streets to show off their paces to prospective buyers, and a sale is confirmed with the traditional gipsy hand-slap.

Mitcham, Surrey

Mitcham Fair has no charter. The earliest record of it is 1732, when it was important for the sale of horses and cattle.

It is held on August 12th, 13th and 14th on Three Kings Common, and attracts great crowds. The Mayor, Mayoress and the President of the Showmen's Guild are present at the opening, at which a 'golden' key, four and a half feet long, is held up.

Ripon, Yorkshire

Fairs have been held in Ripon since the time of King John, but the only survivor is the one now held in the market-place on the first Saturday in August. The fair is opened by 'St.

Wilfrid' who, with his retinue, rides round the town on a white horse. The real St. Wilfrid returned to Ripon in 681 after being exiled in Rome for many years.

Horse Fair, Lee Gap, Woodkirk, Yorkshire

The Lee Fair is nearly 800 years old and is the most popular Horse Fair in Yorkshire as it is held near the junction of two old roads which link Bradford with Wakefield and Dewsbury with Leeds. The fair was always a favourite with gipsies. Until the eighteenth century it was held continuously from August 24th to September 17th, but only on those actual two dates is there a fair nowadays.

SEPTEMBER

Michaelmas Fair, Bedford, Bedfordshire

The fair is held about September 29th. It was once famous for its hot baked pears which came from Old Warden Abbey.

Plum Harvest Fair, Helston, Cornwall

Held during September, Helston Fair is thought to have a Roman origin. Helston also has a Gooseberry Fair on the third Monday in July and another on Whit Monday.

Summercourt, Cornwall

Summercourt has the oldest charter fair in Cornwall, held on September 25th.

Crab Fair, Egremont, Cumberland

The fair is held on the Saturday nearest to September 18th. Once it was the custom of the Lord of the Manor to distribute largesse to the crowd as he rode round the fair. Now crab apples have taken the place of money, and are scrambled for. At this fair a 'gurning' competition is held. Each competitor puts his head through a horse-collar and pulls the ugliest face he can.

St. Giles's Fair, Barnstaple, Devon

St. Giles's is a charter fair held on the Wednesday before September 20th, and for the two following days. It is opened at midday at a ceremony performed at the Guildhall. The Senior Beadle has brewed spiced ale from an Elizabethan recipe; it is poured into silver cups which are part of the Borough plate, and a toast is drunk to the success of the fair. With the ale goes toast and cheese and gingerbread.

After the ceremony the civic authorities and their guests go to the Strand, and from the steps of Queen's Walk the Town Clerk declares the fair open. A white glove, decorated with dahlias and ribbons, is hung over one of the Guildhall windows. The first day of the fair is for horse-dealing, the second for cattle, and the third for pleasure only.

St. Giles's Fair has been held continuously for 700 years. It is claimed that Athelstan, the grandson of Alfred the Great, gave the town its charter in the tenth century.

Widecombe Fair, Widecombe, Devon

Widecombe Fair is probably the most famous fair in the world, made so by the song which begins 'Tom Pearce, Tom Pearce, lend me your grey mare. . . .' The last line of the chorus mentions 'Old Uncle Tom Cobley and all. . . .' There was an

actual Thomas Cobley who died in 1794 at the age of 96. But as the first record of Widecombe Fair was in 1850, when it was started for the sale of Dartmoor ponies, it seems that its fame has been gained by false pretences. The fair, however, still attracts huge crowds. It is now chiefly a pleasure fair, though some ponies and sheep from Dartmoor are sold. It is held on the second Tuesday in September.

Pony Fair, Barnet, Hertfordshire

The fair is held during the first weekend in September, and has been famous for 700 years. At one time cattle and horses were brought from as far afield as Scotland and Ireland, and as many as 45,000 animals have been sold at one fair. Nowadays the number is hundreds rather than thousands.

St. Giles's Fair, Oxford, Oxfordshire

Once an important trade fair, St. Giles's is the largest surviving fair without a charter. It is held early in September, and has been, with few breaks, for over eight hundred years. It has, in fact, outlived the four charter fairs which the city once had.

St. Giles's Fair began as the wake festival of Walton parish, before Oxford became a University city, and it still occupies its original site in St. Giles and Magdalen Street. St. Giles is the patron saint of cripples, and the story is that, as cripples and beggars were unwelcome visitors to cities, the fair was sited outside the walls.

St. Matthew's Fair, Bridgwater, Somerset

The fair is held during the third week in September, beginning on the Wednesday nearest September 21st, St. Matthew's Day, and lasts for four days. Exmoor ponies and cattle are sold on the first day only.

Cheese Fair, Frome, Somerset

Frome Fair has no special date; it is held sometime during September. Before the cheeses are sold they have to be 'christened' in the River Frome.

Pony Fair, Brough Hill, Westmorland

The fair, held towards the end of September, is probably of Roman origin. It is attended by many gipsies, and is famous for the sale of unbroken ponies from the fells and dales.

Sheep Fair, Wilton, Wiltshire

Wilton has three fairs, held on the second Thursdays in August, September and October. Their charters were granted by Henry VI in 1443. The September fair, known as the Great Fair, was the largest of the three, and even today there is a substantial trade in sheep, though it is not nearly as great as in the nineteenth century.

OCTOBER

Michaelmas Fair, Abingdon, Berkshire

The third of Abingdon's fairs was the Hiring Fair, held on the Monday preceding October 10th, and was popular with dairymaids who were looking for a situation.

Goose Fair, Tavistock, Devon

Tavistock was granted a charter in 1105. The fair is held on the second Wednesday in October, and geese are now conspicuous by their absence.

Pack Monday Fair, Sherborne, Dorset

Pack Monday Fair is the only survivor of Sherborne's three fairs. It takes place on the Monday after Old Michaelmas Day, October 10th, and used to be called St. Michael's Fair. Until quite recently, a band of young people used to march through the streets of the town soon after midnight, making an unearthly noise with tin cans, dustbin lids, teatrays, bugles, horns and whistles. This was known as Teddy Roe's Band.

The story which is believed locally is that Teddy Roe was the foreman mason employed in the re-building of Sherborne Abbey Church after it had been damaged by fire in the late fifteenth century. When, in 1490, the last of the fan-vaulting was completed, Teddy Roe and his workmen packed up their tools (hence 'Pack' Monday) and marched through the streets to announce their achievement. An earlier origin of the custom, however, might be the frightening away of evil spirits during a pagan festival. Teddy Roe's Band became the excuse for hooliganism, unfortunately, and was suppressed by the police.

Barton Fair and Ox-roasting, Tewkesbury, Gloucestershire

This takes place on October 10th, except when the date falls on a Sunday. The town's charter dates from the end of the eleventh century. In 1651 the gates of the monastery, before which the fair was held, were demolished, and the fair moved into the town.

Petersfield, Hampshire

Formerly known as the Taro Fair, it is held on October 6th. In the morning, horses are sold; the rest of the day is given up to pleasure.

Weyhill Fair, near Andover, Hampshire

In its heyday Weyhill Fair saw £300,000 worth of business in sheep transacted on Old Michaelmas Day, October 10th. It is one of the oldest fairs in the country. It is held on a hill-top site where the Tin Road from Cornwall and the Gold Road from Wales meet six other roads at the boundary of three parishes; that has been the site since the eleventh century. It is probable that the fair has an even longer history, going back to pre-Christian times when sacrifices were made at pagan festivals.

Sheep Fair, Leicester, Leicestershire

Leicester's annual fair is held on the Thursday preceding the second Friday in October. It is still important for the sale of sheep.

Goose Fair, Nottingham, Nottinghamshire

Edward I granted the fair's charter in 1284. During the Middle Ages over 20,000 geese were on sale during the three weeks that the fair lasted. They were driven to Nottingham from Lincolnshire and Norfolk, often taking weeks to get there. Not a goose is now seen at the fair, which is devoted wholly to pleasure during the first Thursday, Friday and Saturday in October. The fair was once held in the market-place, but was transferred to the Forest Recreation Ground.

Sloe Fair, Chichester, Sussex

The fair has been held on the Feast of St. Faith (October 6th) since 1108. It was originally called the Bishop's Fair; its present name comes from a sloe tree which used to stand in Oaklands Road, where the fair is held.

Mop Fair, Stratford-upon-Avon, Warwickshire

Held on October 12th, Mop Fair is no longer a hiring fair, but is given over to pleasure. It started in the reign of Edward III and up till the nineteenth century was concerned chiefly with the hiring of servants. Certain old traditions are still kept up, such as ox-roasting and country dancing. It is opened by the Mayor, in his robes and chain of office, preceded by Mace-bearers and the Town Crier.

A Runaway Mop Fair is held later in the month.

Mop Fair, Warwick, Warwickshire

The traditional date for Warwick's fair is October 12th, and it continues for the two following Saturdays. It is still held near its original site by the market-place. Like Stratford's fair, it was formerly a hiring fair, turning into a pleasure fair during the last century. At the end of October there is a Runaway Mop Fair.

Mop Fair, Marlborough, Wiltshire

Marlborough has two fairs, the Small Mop and the Large Mop. The former is held on the Saturday before Old Michaelmas Day, the latter on the Saturday after Old Michaelmas Day.

Cheese Fair, Yarm, Yorkshire

Yarm's fair was granted its charter by King John in 1216. It is held for three days during October and, though chiefly a pleasure fair, horses may still be bought; the fair is attended by many gipsies.

NOVEMBER

Glove Fair, Truro, Cornwall

This is a one-day fair, held on November 18th.

Martinmas Hiring Fair, Ulverston, Lancashire

Now only a pleasure fair, it is held on The Gills about November 11th.

DECEMBER

Beast Mart, Boston, Lincolnshire

The fair is officially proclaimed open every year about December 10th. Sheep are still sold there although pleasure is the chief commodity.

Cattle Fair, Leicester, Leicestershire

The December Cattle Fair is one of four held on the second Thursday of a month, the others being March, May and July. Another takes place on the second Friday in October. With the Sheep Fair in October, Leicester is well supplied with fairs.

EASTER AND WHITSUN

Cornwall is especially rich in fairs at this time of the year. Helston has one on Whit Monday, Kilkhampton on the Thursday before Holy Thursday; Lanreath has one during the third week after Shrove Tuesday and another on Whit Tuesday.

Roche's May Fair is held on the Wednesday before Ascension Day, and Truro has one on the Wednesday in Whit week.

Easter Monday fairs are held at Bakewell in Derbyshire, Durham in County Durham, Southampton in Hampshire, and Blackburn in Lancashire. Bakewell has another fair on Whit Monday, and on that day there are also fairs at Barnard Castle in County Durham, Watford in Hertfordshire, Preston and Ulverston in Lancashire, and on Hampstead Heath in London. During Whit week they can be found at Kingsteignton in Devon, Chipping Campden in Gloucestershire, Pinner in Middlesex, Tamworth in Staffordshire, Long Melford in Suffolk, and Broadway in Worcestershire.

Stamford and Grantham in Lincolnshire both hold their fair halfway through Lent; Wells in Norfolk and Lichfield in Staffordshire have chosen Shrove Tuesday.

Trinity Fair, Southwold, Suffolk

Henry VII granted a charter for the fair in 1485, and it is opened every Trinity Sunday by the Mayor. As the original charter was destroyed by fire the Town Crier reads another, which was granted by William IV, from the steps of a roundabout, and the Mayor's party enjoys the first ride. The proclamation is also read from the High Street and from the marketplace.

Rothwell, Northamptonshire

Rothwell's fair, which is one of the largest in the county, is held during the week following Trinity Sunday, and is opened by the agent of the Lord of the Manor at 6 a.m. on Monday. He rides on horseback from the Manor House to the Market House, where he reads the proclamation. Halberdiers and a band accompany him.

Pole or Poll Fair, Corby, Northamptonshire

This is a charter fair, and is most unusual in that it is held only every twenty years, on Whit Monday. Its next appearance should be in 1982. Queen Elizabeth I granted Corby a charter in 1585 after being rescued from a bog, into which her horse had thrown her, by a party of men from Corby who witnessed the incident. The charter was later confirmed by Charles II. The Rector of Corby and the Chairman of the Urban District Council open the fair by a reading of the charter.

The villagers of Corby still keep up an old custom which is unique in the history of fairs. Before the fair opens every road into the village is barred by gates, and visitors are allowed to enter only if they are willing to pay a minimum toll of a few pence. If they are not willing, but insistent on passing through the barrier, they are placed in a chair attached to poles and carried to the village stocks. There they are given another chance to pay the toll. Few refuse a second time, for the penalty is a session in the stocks, there to be made fun of by spectators who have not displayed such obstinacy.

County Calendar

BEDFORDSHIRE

Bedford, *Michaelmas Fair*, September 29th (or near)
Dunstable Downs, *Orange-rolling*, Good Friday
Ickwell, *Maypole Dancing*, May 25th

BERKSHIRE

Abingdon, *St. Mark's Fair*, early May
Electing the Mayor of Ock Street, June 20th (or near)
Michaelmas Fair, Monday before October 10th
Hungerford, *Hocktide Tutti-men*, Second Tuesday after Easter

BUCKINGHAMSHIRE

Eton College, *Wall Game*, November 30th
Fenny Stratford, *Firing the Poppers*, November 11th
High Wycombe, *Weighing the Mayor*, May 20th
Olney, *Pancake Day Race*, Shrove Tuesday

CHESHIRE

> Appleton, *Bawming the Thorn*, July 11th
> Comberbach, *Soul Caking Play*, November 2nd

CORNWALL

> Gulval, St. Mount's Bay, *Blessing of the Mead*, August 24th
> Helston, *Furry Dance*, May 8th
>> *Fair*, Whit Monday
>> *Plum Harvest Fair*, during September
> Kilkhampton, *Fair*, Thursday before Holy Thursday
> Lanreath, *Fair*, Third week after Shrove Tuesday
>> *Fair*, Whit Tuesday
> Marhamchurch, Bude, *Marhamchurch Revel*, Monday after August 12th
> Padstow, *Hobby-horse Festival*, May 1st
> Par, *Enthroning the Boy Bishop*, December 6th
> Roche, *Fair*, Wednesday before Ascension Day
> St. Cleer, Liskeard, *Banishing the Witches*, June 2nd
> St. Columb Major and St. Columb Minor, *Hurling*, Shrove Tuesday
> St. Ives, *Hurling the Silver Ball*, First Monday in February
>> *St. John's Eve Midsummer Bonfires*, June 23rd
> Summercourt, *Fair*, September 25th
> Truro, *Fair*, Wednesday in Whit Week
>> *Glove Fair*, November 18th

COUNTY DURHAM

> Barnard Castle, *Fair*, Whit Monday
> Durham, *Fair*, Easter Monday
> Sedgefield, *Shrovetide Football*, Shrove Tuesday

CUMBERLAND

> Egremont, *Crab Fair*, Saturday nearest September 18th

DERBYSHIRE

> Ashbourne, *Shrovetide Football*, Shrove Tuesday
> Bakewell, *Fair*, Easter Monday
>> *Fair*, Whit Monday

Barlow, *Well-dressing*, Wednesday after August 10th
Buxton, *Well-dressing*, Thursday nearest June 24th
Castleton, *Garland Day*, May 29th
Eyam, *Well-dressing*, Last week in August
       Plague Sunday, Last Sunday in August
Hope, *Well-dressing*, Last Saturday in June (usually)
Stoney Middleton, *Well-dressing*, Saturday before Old August Bank Holiday
Tideswell, *Well-dressing*, Last Saturday in June (usually)
Tissington, *Well-dressing*, Ascension Day
Wirksworth, *Well-dressing*, Whit Saturday
Youlgreave, *Well-dressing*, Saturday nearest June 24th

DEVON

Ashburton, *Ale Tasting*, November 26th
Barnstaple, *St. Giles's Fair*, Wednesday before September 20th
Bideford, *Beating the Clock Race*, First week in June
Exeter, *Lammas Fair*, Tuesday before the third Wednesday in July
Honiton, *Hot Penny Ceremony and Fair*, Tuesday and Wednesday after July 19th
Kingsteignton, *Ram Fair*, Whit Monday
Shebbear, *Turning the Devil's Boulder*, November 5th
Tavistock, *Goose Fair*, Second Wednesday in October
Widecombe, *Fair*, Second Tuesday in September

DORSET

Abbotsbury, *Garland Day*, May 13th
Corfe Castle, *Shrovetide Football*, Shrove Tuesday
Sherborne, *Pack Monday Fair*, Monday after October 10th

ESSEX

Berden, *Enthroning the Boy Bishop*, December 6th
Colchester, *Opening of the Oyster Fishing Season*, September 1st
       Oyster Festival, October 20th

Dunmow, *Dunmow Flitch Trial*, Whit Monday

Thaxted, *Morris dancing*, Easter, Whitsuntide, Trinity Sunday, Boxing Day

GLOUCESTERSHIRE

Chipping Campden, *Scuttlebrook Wake*, Saturday in Whit Week

Cooper's Hill, Birdlip, *Cheese-rolling*, Whit Monday

Cranham, *Fair*, Second Monday in August

Marshfield, *Paper Boys*, December 26th

Painswick, *Clipping the Church*, Sunday nearest September 19th

St. Briavels, *Bread and Cheese Dole*, Whit Sunday

Stow-on-the-Wold, *Horse Fair*, May 12th

Fair, October 24th

Tewkesbury, *Fair*, October 10th

HAMPSHIRE

Petersfield, *Fair*, October 6th

Southampton, *Fair*, Easter Monday

Tichborne and Cheriton, Alresford, *The Tichborne Dole*, March 25th

Weyhill, Andover, *Fair*, October 10th

HEREFORDSHIRE

Hentland, Sellack and King's Capel, near Ross-on-Wye, *Pax Cakes Distribution*, Palm Sunday

Hereford, *St. Ethelbert's Fair*, First Wednesday after May 2nd

HERTFORDSHIRE

Barnet, *Pony Fair*, First weekend in September

Watford, *Fair*, Whit Monday

HUNTINGDONSHIRE

St. Ives, *Dicing for Bibles*, Whit Monday

ISLE OF MAN
    St. John's, *Tynwald Ceremony*, July 5th

KENT
    Biddenden, *Biddenden Dole*, Easter Monday

LANCASHIRE
    Ashton-under-Lyne, *Pageant of the Black Knight*, September 25th
    Bacup, *Nutters Dance*, Easter Saturday
    Blackburn, *Fair*, Easter Monday
    Preston, *Pace-egging*, Easter Monday
              Fair, Whit Monday
    Ulverston, *Fair*, Whit Monday
              Martinmas Hiring Fair, November 11th (or near)
    Warrington, *Walking Day*, June 28th

LEICESTERSHIRE
    Hallaton, *Bottle-kicking and Hare Pie-scrambling*, Easter Monday
    Leicester, *Cattle Fair*, Second Thursday in March, May, July, December, and second Friday in October
              Sheep Fair, Thursday before the second Friday in October

LINCOLNSHIRE
    Boston, *Beast Mart*, December 10th (or near)
    Brigg, *Horse Fair*, August 5th
    Haxey, *Hood Game*, January 6th
    Lincoln, *Fair*, April (one week)
    North Somercotes, *Pancake Day Race*, Shrove Tuesday
    Old Bolingbroke, *Candle Auction*, December 21st

LONDON
    Great Hall of the Guildhall, *Election of Sheriffs*, June 24th
    Hampstead Heath, *Fair*, Whit Monday
    Horse Guards Parade, Whitehall, *Trooping the Colour*,

Second Saturday in June

Guildhall, *Election of the Lord Mayor*, September 29th

Guildhall, *Installation of the Lord Mayor*, November 8th

London Bridge to Chelsea Bridge, *Doggett's Coat and Badge Race*, August 1st (or near)

Mansion House, *The Knollys Red Rose Rent*, June 24th

Mansion House, Guildhall, Law Courts, *Lord Mayor's Show*, Second Saturday in November

Marble Arch, *The Tyburn Walk*, Last Sunday in April

Newgate to Mansion House, *Christ's Hospital Boys' March*, September 21st (or near)

Royal Courts of Justice, Strand, *Horseshoes and Nails Rent*, Between Martinmas and Michaelmas

Royal Hospital, Chelsea, *Founder's Day*, May 29th

St. Andrew Undershaft's Church, Leadenhall Street, *John Stow's Quill Pen Ceremony*, April 5th (or near)

St. Bartholomew the Great's Church, Smithfield, *Poor Widows' Charity*, Good Friday

St. Botolph's Church, Aldgate, *Sir John Cass Commemoration Service*, February 20th (or near)

St. Etheldreda's Church, Ely Place, Holborn, *Blessing of the Throats*, February 3rd

St. James's Palace (Chapel Royal), *Royal Epiphany Gifts*, January 6th

St. Mary-at-Hill Church, *Fish Harvest Festival*, First Sunday in October

St. Paul's Cathedral, *Cakes and Ale Sermon*, Ash Wednesday

Thames, between London and Henley, *Swan Upping*, Last Monday in July (or near)

Theatre Royal, Drury Lane, *Cutting the Baddeley Cake*, January 5th

Upper Thames Street, *Vintners' Procession*, Thursday after July 4th

Wakefield Tower, Tower of London, *Ceremony of the Lilies and the Roses*, May 21st

Westminster Abbey, *Royal Maundy*, Maundy Thursday

Westminster School, *Pancake Greaze*, Shrove Tuesday

Whitehall, *Charles I Commemoration*, January 30th

NORFOLK

>King's Lynn, *Fair*, February 14th
>
>Wells, *Fair*, Shrove Tuesday

NORTHAMPTONSHIRE

>Corby, *Pole Fair*, Whit Monday (every 20 years)
>
>Rothwell, *Fair*, Week following Trinity Sunday

NORTHUMBERLAND

>Allendale, *Tar Burning*, December 31st
>
>Alnwick, *Shrovetide Football*, Shrove Tuesday
>
>Whalton, *Baal Fire*, July 4th

NOTTINGHAMSHIRE

>Blidworth, *Cradle Rocking*, February 2nd (or Sunday nearest)
>
>Edwinstowe, *Enthroning the Boy Bishop*, December 6th
>
>Laxton, *Court Leet*, November 23rd
>
>Nottingham, *Goose Fair*, First Thursday, Friday and Saturday in October

OXFORDSHIRE

>Bampton, *Morris dancing*, Whit Monday
>
>Magdalen College Tower, Oxford, *May Morning Service*, May 1st
>
>Oxford, *St. Giles's Fair*, Early September

SOMERSET

>Bridgwater, *Bonfire Night Celebrations*, November 5th
>
>   *St. Matthew's Fair*, Wednesday nearest September 21st
>
>Carhampton, *Wassailing the Apple Trees*, January 17th
>
>Frome, *Cheese Fair*, During September
>
>Hinton St. George, *Punkie Night*, Last Thursday in October
>
>Minehead, *Hobby-horse Festival*, May 1st
>
>Redcliffe, Bristol, *The Redcliffe Pipe Walk*, October 23rd (or near)

Stoke St. Gregory, *Egg-shackling*, Shrove Tuesday

St. Mary Redcliffe's Church, Bristol, *Rush-bearing*, Whit Sunday

STAFFORDSHIRE

Abbots Bromley, Rugely, *Horn Dance*, First Monday after September 4th

Lichfield, *Fair*, Shrove Tuesday

    Court of Arrays and Greenhill Bower, Whit Monday

    Sheriff's Ride, Saturday nearest September 8th

    Dr. Johnson Commemoration, Saturday nearest September 18th

Tamworth, *Fair*, During Whit week

SUFFOLK

Bury St. Edmunds, *Cakes and Ale Ceremony*, Thursday after Plough Monday

Long Melford, *Fair*, During Whit week

Southwold, *Trinity Fair*, Trinity Sunday

SURREY

Guildford, *Dicing for the Maid's Money*, January 31st

Mitcham, *Fair*, August 12th–14th

SUSSEX

Bodiam, *Pancake Day Race*, Shrove Tuesday

Chichester, *Sloe Fair*, October 6th

Ebernoe, Petworth, *Horn Fair*, July 25th

Findon, *Lamb Fair*, July 14th

    Great Fair, September 14th

Hastings, *Blessing the Sea*, May 26th (or near)

Lewes, *Bonfire Night Celebrations*, November 5th

Rye, *Mayoring Day*, May 23rd

Tinsley Green, Crawley, *Marbles Championship*, Good Friday

WARWICKSHIRE

Atherstone, *Shrovetide Football*, Shrove Tuesday

Knightlow Hill, *Wroth Silver*, November 11th

Meriden, *Great Wardmote of the Woodmen of Arden*, First week in August

Stratford-upon-Avon, *Mop Fair*, October 12th

Warwick, *Mop Fair*, October 12th

WESTMORLAND

Ambleside, *Rush-bearing Festival*, Saturday nearest July 26th

Appleby, *New Fair*, During June

Brough Hill, *Pony Fair*, End of September

Grasmere, *Rush-bearing Festival*, Saturday nearest August 5th

Warcop, *Rush-bearing Festival*, June 29th

WILTSHIRE

Devizes, *Fair*, During April
        Fair, During October

Marlborough, *Small Mop Fair*, Saturday before October 10th
            Large Mop Fair, Saturday after October 10th

Stonehenge, Salisbury Plain, *Druids' Ceremony*, June 23rd

Wilton, *Fair*, Second Thursday in August
       Great Fair, Second Thursday in September
       Fair, Second Thursday in October

Wishford Magna, *Grovely Forest Rights Procession*, May 29th

WORCESTERSHIRE

Broadway, *Fair*, During Whit week

YORKSHIRE

Boyes Staith, Whitby, *Planting the Penny Hedge*, Ascension Eve

Bradford, *Fair*, June 8th–10th
         Fair, June 29th–July 1st

Dewsbury, *Tolling the Devil's Knell*, December 24th

Lee Gap, Woodkirk, *Horse Fair*, August 24th
      Horse Fair, September 17th
Richmond, *First Fruits of the Harvest*, September 19th
Ripon, *Feast of St. Wilfrid*, First Saturday in August
South Dalton, *Kipling Cotes Derby*, Third Thursday in March
Sowerby Bridge (Midgley), *Pace-egg Play*, Good Friday
Yarm, *Cheese Fair*, During October

NORTHERN IRELAND

Belfast, *Battle of the Boyne Celebrations*, July 12th
Londonderry, *Battle of the Boyne Celebrations*, July 12th
     Closing the Gates Ceremony, December 18th
Omagh, *Battle of the Boyne Celebrations*, July 12th

SCOTLAND

KINCARDINESHIRE
  Stonehaven, *Swinging the Fireballs*, December 31st

LANARKSHIRE
  Lanark, *Whuppity Scoorie*, March 1st
    Lanimer Day, Thursday of week June 6th–12th

MIDLOTHIAN
  Musselburgh, *Fishermen's Walk*, Second Friday in September

MORAYSHIRE
  Burghead, *Burning the Clavie*, January 12th

PEEBLESSHIRE
  Innerleithen, *Cleiking the Devil*, Third week in August
  Peebles, *Beltane Festival*, Mid-June

PERTHSHIRE
  Comrie, *Flambeaux Procession*, December 31st

Roxburghshire
>   Hawick, *Riding the Marches*, Thursday of first full week in June
>   Jedburgh, *Fastern E'en Ba'*, First Tuesday after the new moon following February 2nd
>   Melrose, *Freemasons' Walk*, December 27th
>   Souden, *Battle of Otterburn Commemoration*, Second Sunday in August

Selkirkshire
>   Galashiels, *Braw Lads' Gathering*, June 30th
>   Selkirk, *Riding the Marches*, Thursday of first full week in June

Shetland Islands
>   Lerwick, *Up-Helly-Aa'*, Last Tuesday in January

West Lothian
>   South Queensferry, *The Burry Man*, July 8th

WALES

Carmarthenshire
>   Laugharne, *Common Walk*, Whit Monday

Glamorganshire
>   Llangynwyd, *Mari Lwyd Mummers*, December 31st

Site Varies
>   *Royal National Eisteddfod of Wales*, First week in August

(Since the change to Spring Bank Holiday, all 'Whit Monday' events now take place on the last Monday in May.)

Index

Index